Myths
and Legends
of the
Ancient Near East

Books by Fred Gladstone Bratton

HISTORY OF EGYPTIAN ARCHAEOLOGY

HISTORY OF THE BIBLE

LEGACY OF THE LIBERAL SPIRIT

MAIMONIDES: MEDIEVAL MODERNIST

MYTHS AND LEGENDS OF THE ANCIENT NEAR EAST

THE FIRST HERETIC: THE LIFE AND TIMES
OF IKHNATON THE KING

THE CRIME OF CHRISTENDOM

Myths
and Legends
of the
Ancient Near East

by

FRED GLADSTONE BRATTON

THOMAS Y. CROWELL COMPANY
NEW YORK
ESTABLISHED 1834

Designed by Ruth Smerechniak

Manufactured in the United States of America

L.C. Card 79-101938
2 3 4 5 6 7 8 9 10

PREFACE

Most of the stories narrated in this book are some four thousand years old. They are from Near Eastern civilizations that were ancient when Israel, Greece, and Rome came upon the scene, but unlike the Bible, the *Odyssey*, and the *Aeneid* they have not been known until comparatively recent times. Our knowledge of these myths had to wait upon the discovery of the tablets and papyri on which they were written and, further, upon their decipherment. This knowledge has been greatly augmented by the recent discovery of hitherto unknown texts—documents confirming the belief of many scholars that myth and ritual were closely allied and that the latter usually preceded the former. In view of the current renewed interest of theologians in mythology, it is now necessary to place a new emphasis on both the discovery of the texts and their translation.

In the case of preliterate cultures we are mainly dependent on archaeological remains for our knowledge. Since no texts are available, we have to study prehistoric periods through artifacts. For many years this also was the only means of studying the literate cultures of the ancient Near East. It was only after the decipherment of strange scripts that we came to know the history and thought of the Egyptians, the Babylonians, the Assyrians, the Hittites, the Cretans, and the Canaanites. "A lost civilization," as Leo Deuel observes, "no matter how splendid the monuments it may yield to the excavator, reveals its inner fabric only through written documents." It is only through the decipherment of these ancient texts that the breakthrough in the reconstruction of history is possible.

The potsherds and tools of Neolithic cultures are obviously more important than the pottery of the later historic Egyptian and Sumerian civilizations because prehistoric cultures left no texts, whereas literate cultures after 3000 B.C. provided an abundance of inscriptions that contain more valuable material than artifacts do. Thus, in many instances newly found texts demand a revision of previously held theories. Dissimilar architectural remains, for instance, might easily indicate two different periods of time, but literary evidence might show that these monuments, though different, belong to the same period.

Illustrations of the revolutionary effect of newly discovered texts on scholarly opinion are many and varied:

the Ugaritic literature, which provides literary evidence that both the Hebrew and Greek writings were dependent upon it; the cuneiform tablets of Boghazköy, which brought to light a corpus of Hittite myths of Babylonian and Hurrian origin and showed that the same myths existed in several Hittite languages; Egyptian hieroglyphic Pyramid Texts, which are inscribed on the walls of the Sakkara pyramids from the third millennium B.C. and which deal with immortality rites; the Coffin Texts from the Middle Kingdom, which contain the Osirian myth; the Theban Book of the Dead from the New Kingdom; and the Theban and Fayum papyri; the cuneiform tablets from the palace of Ashurbanipal in Nineveh, which gave us the great Sumerian and Akkadian epics; the Dead Sea Scrolls from the Judean caves, which revealed a wealth of important information about sectarian Judaism and the close relation of early Christianity to its Judaic parent religion.

The cultural interrelatedness of Egypt, Mesopotamia, Asia Minor, Syria, Palestine, and Crete cannot be questioned, especially in the field of myth and ritual, so that this region can be studied as a whole. All of these areas had the mythology and ritual of the mother goddess, the fertility rites, the vegetation cultus, the creation myth, the myths of death, resurrection, and immortality. The findings of the archaeologists and the translations of the epigraphists have clearly demonstrated the underlying cultural interdependence in mythology of all Near Eastern civilizations since the Neolithic age.

How are we to explain the universal character of the myths and the presence of the same motifs in all these cultures? It is probably due both to diffusion by migration and to the fact that societies during the same phase of evolution, in similar situations, develop similar ideas. However, the presence of verbatim similarity in documents from widely separated countries would point to an actual borrowing of written traditions.

This book is not addressed to the specialist. References and footnotes are therefore kept at a minimum. My aim is to place before the general reader a definitive and comprehensive account of the mythological literature of the four chief cultures of the ancient Near East. The legends and epics of these civilizations have usually been presented in a technical manner and dealt with chiefly because of their relation to the Old Testament. This relationship is indeed important in the case of the Babylonian, Canaanite, and Hittite literatures, although they can be considered in their own right as stories of origins or adventure. The Egyptian stories had less influence on Hebrew literature. "The Legend of Creation" and "The Feud Between Horus and Seth" are myths of the gods and divine origins, but such stories as "The Tale of the Two Brothers" and "The Shipwrecked Sailor" are only semi-mythological fairy tales. Many of the ancient myths were written for entertainment purposes only and are more secular than religious.

The exclusion of Israel from a survey of the mythology of the ancient Near East may be surprising to some readers but it is largely because Hebrew literature appeared comparatively late and its mythical features were a result rather than a source of ancient Near Eastern mythology. Further, the dependence of the Hebrews on Sumerian, Akkadian, and Canaanite mythical traditions such as the creation and flood stories is fairly well known. The borrowing of myths and thought-forms from earlier cultures by the authors of the Old Testament will be indicated throughout in passing. To go beyond that would necessitate a highly technical textual study of the Pentateuch and a rather fruitless attempt to separate legend from history. Extensive studies of

Hebrew mythology have been made by Raphael Patai: *Hebrew Myths: The Book of Genesis* (with Robert Graves); *Man and Temple in Ancient Jewish Myths and Ritual;* and *The Hebrew Goddess.*

The specimens of literature presented here are taken from tombs, stelae, papyri, pyramids, and clay tablets. The selection of texts has been made with an eye to their literary value, their cultural and theological outlook, their influence on later literature, and their moral values. The myths afford us an insight into the intellectual life of these early peoples just as validly as historical data.

Whoever attempts to write about the literature of the ancient Near East is inevitably indebted to such authorities as John A. Wilson, Rudolf Anthes, James H. Breasted, Alexandre Piankoff, Henri Frankfort, Flinders Petrie, Adolf Erman, E. A. Wallis Budge, Alan H. Gardiner, Kurt Sethe, Samuel Noah Kramer, Stephen Langdon, Thorkild Jacobsen, C. L. Woolley, Theodor H. Gaster, James B. Pritchard, E. A. Speiser, A. Heidel, L. W. King, Albrecht Goetze, H. G. Güterbock, H. L. Ginsberg, Cyrus H. Gordon, A. S. Kapelrud, C. F. Pfeiffer, J. Obermann, O. R. Gurney, G. R. Driver, J. Gray, and C. F. Schaeffer for their scholarly contributions in translation and research. In the preparation of this volume I have found their works indispensable.

Translations of Sumerian, Akkadian, Egyptian, Ugaritic, and Hittite original tablets and papyri have been made by a number of epigraphists and vary considerably. The translations presented in this volume are modernized and popularized (and in some instances shortened) versions. For the sake of intelligibility restorations have been made where necessary and repetitious material omitted. The *Sumerian-Akkadian* stories are based on the translations of the following scholars, to whom I express my indebtedness: E. A.

Speiser, Stephen Langdon, and Samuel Noah Kramer; *Egyptian:* John A. Wilson, Rudolf Anthes, E. A. Wallis Budge, Adolf Erman, James H. Breasted, Flinders Petrie, and F. Ll. Griffith; *Ugaritic-Canaanite:* H. L. Ginsberg, Cyrus H. Gordon, and T. H. Gaster; *Hittite:* Albrecht Goetze, H. G. Güterbock, and T. H. Gaster.

Here and there the reader may be confused by apparent inconsistencies in names of deities. This is due to the fact that the names and the gods themselves in many instances are interchangeable.

My hope is that this small book will help the reader find a new appreciation of the literary interdependence of all early cultures and, to a surprising degree, their contemporaneousness.

FRED GLADSTONE BRATTON

CONTENTS

PANTHEON CHARTS

MAP

PHOTOGRAPHS

Following page 74

Female figurine from Tepe Gawra, northern Mesopotamia
Head of goddess Ningal, from Ur
Sumerian seal showing sun god Shamash
Inlay of goddess Astarte from Khorsabad, Assyria
Part of Tablet XI of the Gilgamesh epic, from Assyria
Tablet giving Babylonian version of creation, from
Nineveh
Relief slab with Sumerian goddess Ishtar
Egyptian scribe holding roll of papyrus, from Sakkara
Statuettte of Maat, Egyptian goddess of truth and justice
Adoration of the sun, from Book of the Dead, Hunefer
Papyrus

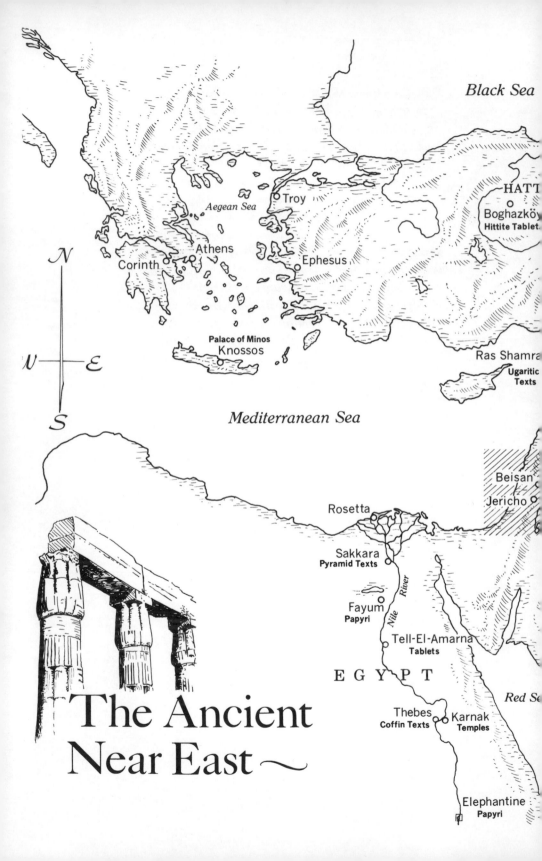

Black Sea

HATT

Boghazköy
Hittite Tablet.

Aegean Sea

Troy

Athens

Corinth

Ephesus

Ras Shamra
Ugaritic Texts

Palace of Minos
Knossos

Mediterranean Sea

Beisan

Jericho

Rosetta

Sakkara
Pyramid Texts

Nile River

Fayum
Papyri

Tell-El-Amarna
Tablets

E G Y P T

Red Se

Thebes
Coffin Texts

Karnak
Temples

The Ancient
Near East ～

Elephantine
Papyri

Caspian Sea

AKKAD

Euphrates

Tigris River

River

Nineveh
Flood Tablets

Nuzi

Behistun

Baghdad

Babylon

Kish

SUMER

Lagash

Susa
Code of Hammurabi

Ur
Royal Tombs

ARABIA

Persian Gulf

Don Pitcher

Megiddo
Solomon's
Stables

Beisan
Temple of Dagon

Jericho

Jerusalem

Gilgal

Qumran
Scrolls

CANAAN

Dead Sea

0   50   100   150   200   250
Scale of Miles

INTRODUCTION:
The Nature and
Meaning of Myth

ALLEGORY OR SUPERSTITION?

The imaginative stories of children, when they sponta-
neously try to account for some occurrence or phenome-
non beyond their knowledge, are a reenactment of mythmaking among primitive men. In the childhood of the race
men wondered how the world, or what they knew of it,
was created, and where and how man came into being.
Later, they pondered the more profound questions of
justice and morals, life and death.

All early civilizations inherited this attempt by primi-
tives to deal with these problems, with the result that the
myth became a universal possession among ancient cul-

tures. Oddly enough, whenever men have sought for some set of values or revelation of truth upon which to base their lives, they have resorted not to history but to ageless myth. Myths were used as the explanatory narratives accompanying religious rites but often they were simply tales that were told orally from generation to generation and simplified or changed with each telling. The myth came into being to lend authority and divine sanction to the customs, beliefs, and rituals of the group. Mythology was the ancient man's science; by it, he explained to the best of his ability the origin and nature of God, man, and the universe—the same problems that preoccupy the minds of philosophers today. Myths developed also as explanations of the aberrations and inequalities of society. The insecurity of life, the frailties of men, and the mystery of death inevitably led to legends about gods and heroes, heaven and the future life. The activities of the gods simply mirrored the organization of human family life: father, mother, brother, sister; and each deity had his or her own function or sphere of activity. The rituals enacted by the people were a reminder to the fertility god of the necessity of fecundity, or they took the form of a celebration before the god of the hereafter, of the renewal of life in man and in the soil.

There is a diversity of opinion among the experts on the meaning of ancient myths. Some scholars dismiss them as the naive fairy tales of primitive man, the fantastic superstitions of uninformed people. Others see in them profound insights about the cosmos and life, directly perceived, unencumbered by the restrictions of modern logic. Many theologians and historians regard myths as symbols or allegories representing great truths—imaginative stories, intentionally fictitious, employed to explain to common people the origin of the universe, the activities of the gods, and the moral dilemmas of man. Opposing this last view are those historians who feel that the ancients, living in a world of magic and miracle, believed implicitly in their stories as factual, and they further state that ancient writers could not have been sufficiently sophisticated to write symbolically. Many identify ancient myths with cultic ritual—explanations of the performed rites. The myth may precede the ritual or follow it. Sometimes a myth is borrowed from an earlier culture and placed in a new context with new implications.

It can be said that all myths to a certain degree are symbolic and ritualistic. They are an interpretation of life from a suprahistorical point of view: the sacred tradition of a given culture. The fact that an event may have occurred in history does not exclude the mythologizing of that event or the interpretation of it as a symbol of a belief. An example of a recent event becoming a myth in one generation is the Mao revolution in China. The new tradition developed around the "Long March," or retreat, of the Chinese Communists in 1934–35.[1] This was a historical occurrence that became mythologized in the form of an epic story. The divine hero was Mao Tse-tung, who gave his people a new revelation in the holy book to which all his followers, led by the army, were committed. The event thus became a mythological symbol representing the new way of life.

Another example of the mythologizing of a historical event is the Akkadian flood story. Excavations at Ur and Kish in Iraq, starting in 1929, showed that an unprecedented inundation of the Tigris-Euphrates valley actually occurred about 4000 B.C. (and a later one about 3300 B.C.). The story was handed down and ultimately became one of the Sumerian legends independent of the actual event. Eventually the myth became part of the Gilgamesh epic of Akkadian mythology.

The New Testament belief in the Resurrection might

well be considered as a mythological symbol of the victory of life over death, as well as proof of the justice and righteousness of God. Resurrection thus vindicates the good life and proves that the stars in their courses are on the side of right. It is also seen as a reward for goodness, offering compensation for the suffering of the righteous on earth. This conviction was personalized in the story of Jesus' resurrection, which, for the early Christians at least, was evidence of God's intervention in history. The idea of resurrection had already existed in Pharisaic doctrine. It continued in Christianity as a combination of myth and history—for some a historical fact, however interpreted, and for others a symbolic myth.

The problem of myth is not a modern development. It occupied the minds of the Greeks, who were concerned with the relation of rationalism to traditional beliefs. The Sophists and Neoplatonists anticipated one modern solution by defining myths as allegories that symbolized moral or spiritual truth and were not to be taken literally. The Neoplatonic and Stoic philosophers of the Hellenistic period were thus able to hold both to tradition and rationalism. This method of interpretation was rejected by Plato and the later Epicureans as just a way of keeping intact the traditional supernatural beliefs of the state religion and keeping the facts of history from the people. The emperor Julian regarded myths as esoteric teachings understood only by the intellectual aristocracy. The early Christian theologians discredited the pagan myths while teaching new ones for the Hebrew and Christian religions.

The Christian Humanists of the Italian Renaissance were more tolerant of classic myths, regarding them as allegories of moral ideals. Christian artists used Greek and Roman mythological figures to convey religious and secular ideas. The Rationalists of the French Enlightenment flatly rejected myths as superstition. In their devotion to reason, it might be added, they also rejected much of Hebrew and Christian Scripture.

A reaction to rationalism occurred in the late eighteenth and early nineteenth century Romantic movement, in which poetic myth was regarded as an independent and authentic field of philosophic thought and as a record of cultural history. This was the view of Friedrich W. J. Schelling (1775–1854), who brought into the discussion a theological point of view. He saw myth not as a fictional symbol but as a part of God's revelational process. It was a necessary step in the developing consciousness of man as he advanced in his conception of God. Ernst Cassirer's *Philosophy of Symbolic Forms* is a modern adaptation of Schelling's interpretation along a more critical and less revelational line. But he insists that myth has its own reality as a "necessary form of the spirit," a unity of structure and function. Thus for Cassirer myth is not just a symbol concealing some spiritual truth but an independent form of reality in its own right. With him the ritual always precedes the myth, which is the narrative explanation of the rite. The rite itself is magically efficacious, a performance in which the person becomes identified with the god. This form of reasoning, in which Cassirer tries to hold to the myth as a self-contained objective reality and at the same time a symbolic interpretation of the rite, leaves something to be desired in the mind of a rationalist or empiricist. It does not rid one of the impression that the myth is only the attempt of the primitive mind to explain the world of the spirit and has no objective reality for the modern thinker. To this Cassirer would reply that the reality of the myth lies in its pragmatic function rather than its objective truth; the myth is a psychological aid rather than an empirical fact. But to claim both objectivity and pragmatic function as an aid to belief is inconsistent. A more plausible interpretation would be that the myth is either a purely subjective, nonrational mode of thought serving the psychological purpose of fostering and sustaining beliefs or that it represents the uncritical literal acceptance of the factual reality of the legend.

Contemporary theories, too numerous and involved to explore in this volume, include the anthropological approach (Frazer, E. B. Tyler), which, following Hegel, sees the myth as a dialectical stage in the evolution of civilization; the functional interpretation (Malinowski, Bultmann, Berdyaev), which defines myth as a nonintellectual justification of belief and the guarantee of the rite; the instinct or emotion school (Dardel, Lévy-Bruhl, Bergson, Durkheim), which says that myth is a nonrational, nonreflective reaction to reality, the source of religion, an experience "beyond truth and falsity"; the ethnological approach, which interprets myth literally as an expression of primitive thought (Lang); and the collective-unconscious theory (Jung), which holds that the myth originates in dream and phantasy—a view substantiated by the dreams of modern people, which contain the same motifs as ancient mythologies.

The new studies in ethnology, anthropology, psychology, folklore, and religion have all combined to demonstrate, or at least suggest, a spiritually unified world, a common spiritual background for all peoples. There is a danger, however, in claiming that the foundations of our religions and systems of values lie in the realm of the psyche, the unfathomable, rather than in history and human experience. Recent writers have pressed this idea to the point of defining essential Christianity as the celebration of a timeless truth rather than a reliving of a historical event—an experience that possesses "the dignity of myth," something which is beyond all time.[2] According to the new approach to mythology, the attempt to prove the factuality of the myth, as the official creeds do, actually destroys its value. "A God conceptually defined, a Christ believed in as a factual rock, is at once changed from a creative image to a dead idol. The anxiety to believe is the very opposite of faith, of self-surrender to the truth— whatever it is or may turn out to be."[3] In short, mythology divines rather than defines—this is the crux of the contemporary school of interpretation. It is not concerned with how much of the myth is fact and how much fiction, but only with the amount of light it sheds on the inner meaning of life.

Myth in the minds of these scholars is therefore not to be explained from the point of view of folklore or anthropology. The myth is not to be regarded as something untrue or unhistorical but as a revelation of the meaning of life and the universe. To them the anthropological view—that myth comes from the primitive stage in the history of civilization—is quite unsatisfactory because it ignores the highly developed cultures in both pre-Hellenic and non-European ancient times. These so-called early or primitive cultures, it is maintained, were more intelligent than they are given credit for, and their myths were highly sophisticated instruments of truth.

THE PRIMITIVE MIND

A survey of philosophical theories shows that myths are variously regarded as products of a "mythopoeic age"; romantic tales based on historical events; etiological epics explaining natural phenomena; didactic legends with a moral motive; imaginative stories used symbolically or allegorically to explain cosmic events; legends with or without a factual basis used to bolster theological beliefs; or products of primitive mentality, which in its prelogical state could not account for certain events in any other way.

Sophisticated philosophical, psychological, and sociological theories aside, one cannot minimize the historical view, which recognizes the difference between the primitive and the rational mind. Primitive people, ancient or modern, make no distinction between the natural and the supernatural, between nature and man, human experience and cosmic events. They have no knowledge of natural laws or natural causation. Speculation among the ancients could not take an intellectual or rational form; it had to be poetic or imaginative. Theirs was a world of myth, magic, and miracle. In the presence of the unknown and the inexplicable they resorted to the supernatural by way of the mythical explanation or the ritual drama. When famine, flood, or other disasters endangered their lives the strain and tension compelled them to resort to myth and ritual. To account for the creation of man and the world, to insure continuity of life in the Hereafter, to guarantee order in social life and nature, and to give supernatural sanction to the cultic ritual, the myth was a necessary implement.

Myth and ritual promote social cohesion and rapport, continuity of belief, and a sense of security. The sacred rite is reenacted and the story retold as it happened in the beginning. The established ritual, thus rooted in ancient precedent, gains stability and permanence. This explanation of ancient myth and ritual obviously applies to modern cultures. The majority of Christians throughout the world today are held to their religious beliefs by this same psychological means—as seen in the biblical stories, the creeds, the ritual of the sacred meal, and religious festivals. The consciousness that the "uttered rite" and the commonly held beliefs have been transmitted for centuries and are observed in the same way throughout the world gives to the believer a sense of efficacy and permanence.

Closely related to the true myth but less vital to the cultural life of the community are the folk tale and the fairy tale. The purpose of the folk legend is entertainment, although in some cases it may be considered a remnant of the serious myth. Folk stories of past heroes and events were transmitted orally with certain embellishments and then, after having become fairly stabilized in content, were put in writing. The fairy tale, more fictitious and romantic, relies on the supernatural and magical, and usually deals with the conflict of good and evil. Like the folk tale, the function of the fairy tale is purely entertainment. The saga or folk legend is part history and part myth. Often, as in the stories of the Trojan War, much of the myth turns out to be history. And frequently, as with the Babylonian flood epic, the story has a factual source—in this case, the local inundation in Mesopotamia in the fourth millennium B.C.

RITUAL AND THE SACRED DRAMA

The cult drama of the fourth and third millennia B.C. in the ancient Near East was centered around the god-king concept and the seasonal festivals in which the death and resurrection of the god were celebrated as symbols of the decay and rebirth of the soil. All these rites had to do with the seasons, the sun, fecundity, immortality, and stability. The Egyptian greeting found in all inscriptions— Life, Health, Strength—typifies this universal preoccupation. The cultic ritual dramatized the myth and gave concrete assurance to the people. Thus ritual and myth are simply aspects of the same sacred rite. The prior and more important element in this confrontation with the supernatural was the drama, for action always precedes belief. Although dogma and tradition occupy an important place in the Christian religion, the ritual practices of early Christianity came before their explanation in creedal form. After the sacred ritual became fixed, it became necessary to justify it and give it supernatural sanction.

The cosmic myths of Egypt, Babylonia, Asia Minor, and Canaan are narratives of what was supposed to have happened in the Dream Times, the primeval days. They were then reenacted in the sacred rites in order to insure fertility, stability, victory over adverse forces, and immortality. The myths tell of the struggles of the gods, the warfare between good and evil powers, the death and resurrection of the vegetation deity. The annual festivals celebrated in symbolic acts the death of the god, the lamentation of the mother goddess, the restoration of the god-king, and the ordeal of entrance into the realm of the Hereafter. These rites were practically the same in all the religions of the ancient Near East.

Thus we see the vital connection between myth and ritual. Their function was not only to record and celebrate past events but to prepare the individual to live effectively in the present in a hazardous and uncertain environment. The myths are often based on historic events and people but more often come from the desire to see order and permanence in the universe. The sacred acts and retold stories served one purpose: to insure the means of subsistence, rapport with the natural and supernatural world, and continuity of life. These hopes and the means of satisfying them, arising from 3000 B.C. to 1000 B.C., were the same throughout the ancient world. The similarity was due to cultural contacts and common circumstances.

According to E. O. James the myth is "a symbolic representation of the Ultimate Reality, however this may be conceived, concerning the essential meaning and facts of existence and of human destinies." [4] "The myth," in

Henri Frankfort's words, "is nothing less than a carefully chosen cloak for abstract thought. . . . It represents the form in which the experience has become conscious." [5] The myth differs from a creed or statement of thought in that it is a concrete story. It is in the mind of the teller a form of poetic truth. Among the early Near Eastern peoples speculative thought took the form of mythology. Myth was the language of religion, and ritual its form of worship. Myth, in the minds of contemporary scholars, is considered a valid aspect of human experience and reality. It is not history but an attempt to define man's relation supernaturally to the spiritual world and the world of values. In a broad sense, it is really a nonempirical method of ascertaining truth. [6]

Considered more critically and from a wider perspective, it might be said that the current preoccupation of theologians with myth is somewhat disproportionate to its importance. It shows a lack of historical balance and philosophical stability, so evident in the credulous manner with which the same scholars seized Neo-Orthodoxy as the wave of the future and rejected the historical point of view as outmoded. It is one thing to see the myth as an ancient means of producing and maintaining faith but to call it an "indispensable" aspect of cosmic truth above and beyond reason is a form of anti-intellectualism otherwise unacceptable to the same scholars. The study of myth as a means of understanding the ancient mentality is proper, but to adopt the myth as a necessary utility for bolstering a shaky theology is to betray the life of reason, man's best hope.

THE UNIVERSALITY OF MYTHIC MOTIFS

Scholars in recent years have been intrigued by the problem of the worldwide distribution of the same themes in mythology. Whether in mere entertainment or in serious religious contexts where they represent ultimate truths, these same motifs exist in all cultures. Although zealous devotees throughout the world blindly worship in their own tradition and dismiss all other systems as false or inadequate, they are all making use of the same few mythological motifs. Each cultural group has interpreted and applied these revelations to its own needs.

Apparently man cannot live without beliefs based on myth. "In fact," writes Joseph Campbell, "the fullness of his life would even seem to stand in a direct ratio to the depth and range, not of his rational thought, but of his local mythology. Why should it be that whenever men had looked for something solid on which to found their lives, they have chosen, not the facts in which the world abounds, but the myths of an immemorial imagination? . . . And it is further true that though people agree in rational terms they are actually driven apart by the self-motivating and self-determining myths to which they cling."[7]

It is clear, as we have previously stated, that the universality of certain mythological ideas is a result of either the same reactions of the human psyche independently to similar situations, the oral spread of these themes geographically with migration, or the literary dependence of one civilization upon another.[8] All three factors must be kept in mind, for although most cultures have evolved from earlier cultures and the myths have thus been diffused, their *continuance* in any society is dependent upon their innate appeal to the human mind.

Creation myths are the most widespread of all myths. Variations occur in the identity of the creator but most of them attribute creation to the sun and some to the process of evolution, and they were not far from being correct. Perhaps it is more accurate to say that although myths of the creation of the world are not found in all areas of the world, stories of the creation of mankind are universal. A. G. Rooth learned that the three hundred creation myths of the North American Indians found by him could be divided into eight types and that seven of the eight occurred also in Eurasia.[9] Maria Leach has edited a collection of sixty-two creation stories from such widely scattered sources as North, South, and Central America; Africa; Oceania; Siberia; and the classic epics of the Near and Far East.[10] One of the noticeable duplications of motifs in practically all of these was the idea that the universe began with chaos on primeval water.

It is natural, in view of early man's curiosity about the universe and the mystery of life itself, that the creation myth should be found everywhere; but it is surprising to find that the flood story is almost as common and is found even in countries where the environment would not logically foster such a reaction. In the recurrence of the flood story throughout the world we must resort to diffusion and borrowing perhaps more than to psychological response. One noteworthy element in most flood stories is that the deluge comes by way of punishment.

An apt illustration of cultural borrowing is the biblical story about the birth and court life of Moses in Egypt (Exod. 2:1–10), which seems to be dependent upon the older legend of Sargon of Agade. Scholars of the liberal school regard the striking similarity as too close to be accidental, but conservative scholars think that the two accounts represent a coincidence. The Sumerian legend runs in part as follows:

> I am Sargon, king of Agade. My lowly mother conceived me and in secret she brought me forth. She set me in a basket of rushes and cast me into the river. The river did not rise over me but bore me and carried me

to Akki the irrigator, who lifted me out and brought
me up as his own son. I became Akki's gardener and
the goddess Ishtar loved me. For four years I ruled the
kingdom.[11]

Other examples of the duplication of mythic motifs, especially in the ancient Near East, are the slaying of
monsters or dragons; incest; the wisdom and divinity of
serpents, bulls, bees, and beetles; paradise; resurrection
and immortality; the underworld; the mother goddess;
the sun, moon, and stars; fratricide; the dying and rising
god; impregnation by a rock, by an animal, or by a god;
virgin birth; the hero, lord, and savior; battle between the
powers of light and the powers of darkness. As we now
proceed to examine the dominant myths of the great civilizations of the ancient Near East, we will encounter
many of these cross-cultural universals.

THE
SUMERO-AKKADIAN
MYTHOLOGY

SUMERO-AKKADIAN PANTHEON

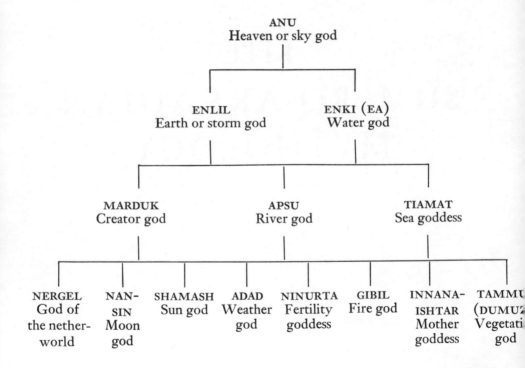

NOTE
*Levels indicate importance, rather than genealogical
descent, of gods.*

The Land of the Two Rivers

Urban civilization made its appearance simultaneously in Egypt and Mesopotamia about 4000 B.C., a development resulting from the formulation of political units, the division of labor into various specialized functions, the invention of writing, and the use of metal. In both countries the immediate impetus was the need for irrigation and maximum use of the water deposited by the annual inundation, a process that necessitated an organized government, written records, and mathematics.

Just as Egypt was the gift of the Nile, so there could not have been a Mesopotamian civilization without the

Tigris-Euphrates. For both countries the annual overflow of the river with its deposit of black silt was the difference between life and death, for it alone enabled the
people along the banks to grow crops and raise cattle.
This was not the only parallel between these two cradles
of civilization. Both were strictly theocratic and authori-
tarian cultures, ruled by god-kings and priests. Since the
gods were really responsible for cosmic order and human
destiny, there could be no sense of history or change. It
was for the common man to accept without question the
rule of divinely appointed priests and kings and to accom-
modate himself to the established order of things. Both
countries had nature gods and celebrated the death and
resurrection of the vegetation deity in the seasonal festivals. Both started with a pictograph system of writing,
which later developed into a shortened alphabetical
form.

On the other hand, there were serious differences between the two lands. Egypt was a homogeneous, unified
country, protected from invasion by natural barriers. As
a result it became the most stable and durable civilization in history and enjoyed a political unity (with brief
interruptions) for over three millennia. Mesopotamia in
the same period (4000–600 B.C.), less isolated and lacking natural protection, experienced a succession of political
regimes, was invaded repeatedly, and really never knew
political stability, although her architecture, art, language, and religion remained constant. Invasions brought
foreign rule, but the conqueror usually fell in with the
ways of those conquered, thus making possible a cultural
continuity. A vital difference between the Mesopotamians
and the Egyptians was in the standard of values. The
Egyptians, while laying great store on the Hereafter, content with an unchanging universe and a theocratic rule,

nevertheless were more optimistic, had more incentive, were saner, happier, and more sensitive to beauty, and followed a higher moral code than their contemporaries to the north.

The debt of the Hebrews to Sumerian religious literature and law is well known to students of the Old Testament. The cuneiform script was used by all Semitic groups, one evidence of its widespread use being the Amarna letters written in Palestine and Syria in the fourteenth century B.C. Along with the borrowing of the system of writing by other nations went the Sumerian culture. Nowhere is the dissemination of Sumerian cosmology and theology more apparent than in Palestine, where the Hebrew Scripture took form. Some fragments of songs probably date back to 1000 B.C., but no actual written material in Hebrew appeared before the ninth century B.C. By that time the Sumerian literary documents from 3000 B.C. to 2000 B.C. were known to the Akkadians of central Mesopotamia, whose Semitic language was used by the Hurrians, the Canaanites, the Hittites, and the Hebrews.

The Sumerian Pantheon

The geographic-climatic factor in the development of cultures cannot be ignored. Environment played an important role in determining the mood or dominant thought of Egypt and Mesopotamia; but whereas it gave to the Egyptian a profound sense of security, it produced just the opposite in the mind of the Babylonian. Here in the Land of the Two Rivers the natural phenomena were not so reliable as in the Nile country. Nature was not so kind: floods were more violent, dust storms more blinding, cloud bursts more torrential. The forces of nature seemed to be opposed to man—were so overpowering, in fact, that he could only bow in submission and repeat with the Hebrew Psalmist: "What is man that thou art mindful of him?" "Man is as wind," said the Sumerians. "A man must obey his god." "Obey those in authority." "Man's life consists in exalting the gods." "O Anu, thy great command takes precedence above all else." Man's crossing the stage of life was of little consequence. Caught in the grasp of cosmic forces he was impressed with his own impotence and his dependence upon the gods. He saw the cosmos as supreme power and authority, ruled by a hierarchy of gods.

It has been estimated that a list of Sumerian deities would contain more than five thousand names. In the scholastic period (from the twenty-fifth to the twenty-third centuries B.C.) the Sumerian theologians systematized the pantheon and gave final form to the temple liturgies and festivals. This theology and its accompanying ritual were accepted as canonical and unchangeable by the later Babylonians and Assyrians and were so held until the fall of Babylonia in 538 B.C.

The oldest trinity of the Sumerian pantheon was that of Anu, the heaven or sky god; Enlil, the earth or storm god; and Enki, the water god, who was associated with Ea. It was the firmament, the all-encompassing sky with its *mysterium tremendum* and its awesome fascination, that awakened in the Mesopotamian the consciousness of the insignificance of human life and, at the same time, the feeling of reverence for the majestic power of Lord Anu. Mere contemplation of the omnipotence of the sky god compelled one's humble submission.

Anu as the god of heaven was called the king of the gods, but his authority carried over into human relations. The celestial order had its counterpart in the mundane world with its hierarchy of authority. The representative

of Anu on earth was the king, whose command was therefore divine. One was taught to obey without question the
orders of the king, the priest, and the head of the family.
All the gods obeyed Anu, "whose command is the very
foundation of heaven and earth." This legal structure in
the cosmic state is defined by Thorkild Jacobsen as the
divine will.

> We see thus that Anu is the source of and active prin-
> ciple in all authority, both in human society and in the
> larger society which is the universe. He is the force
> which lifts it out of chaos and anarchy and makes it
> into a structure, an organized whole; he is the force
> which insures the necessary voluntary obedience to
> orders, laws, and customs in society and to the natural
> laws in the physical world, in short, to world order.
> As a building is supported by, and reveals in its struc-
> ture the lines of, its foundation, so the Mesopotamian
> universe is upheld by, and reflects in *its* structure a
> divine will.[1]

Unlike his father Anu, Enlil took an active interest in
human affairs. He represented the creative element in the
pantheon, having separated heaven from earth, nourished
"the seed of the land," brought forth "whatever was need-
ful" for man, and produced abundance on the earth.

Enki, the water god, was the "Lord of Wisdom," "the
god of civilization." Nergel, the ruler of the netherworld,
was considered the god of pestilence and death. Nan-Sin,
the moon god, was important because of the connection
of the moon's phases with divination and astrology. Shamash (Utu), the sun god, was the god of justice, law,
and order. Adad was the god of weather and rain, fertility,
storms, and floods. Ninurta also was a fertility and solar
deity. Gibil, the fire god, was an exorciser of evil spirits.
Innana-Ishtar, the mother goddess, was the goddess of love
and fertility and the mother of humanity. Tammuz or

Dumuzi, the consort of Innana-Ishtar, was the vegetation god who disappeared in the fall and was resurrected in the spring. He is mentioned in the Old Testament (Ezek. 8:14) as the god of productiveness. The suffering and dying of the god symbolized the cycle of the seasons— death of the soil in the autumn and new life in the spring. Marduk was the creator god of the Babylonian pantheon and Ashur, the chief Assyrian deity.

The Odyssey of Gilgamesh

The Sumerians were the first to compose epic literature in the form of the heroic tale. At least nine such narrative poems have survived through versions written in Akkadian—the Semitic language used by the Babylonians and Assyrians. The Sumerians were a non-Semitic people in lower Mesopotamia. Their cultural importance extended from about 3500 to 2000 B.C., and they wrote in cuneiform characters on clay tablets, some of which date from 4000 B.C. The ancient city-states of Ur, Uruk, Larsa, Lagash, Nippur, and Eridu, situated on the banks of the Euphrates, were the capitals of Sumer. The Semitic dynasty of Akkad was founded by Sargon the Great (2700 B.C.), with Agade as the capital. Eventually the centers of the Mesopotamian civilization moved to Babylon and Nineveh, the capitals of the Babylonian and Assyrian kingdoms.

The Akkadian myths (that is, those of Babylonia and Assyria) come from Sumerian prototypes, with which they are almost identical—the most famous of which is the Gilgamesh epic, which influenced all later Mediterranean literature, including that of the Greeks. The texts for the Gilgamesh epic come from the library of Ashurbanipal (668–626 B.C.). There are also Akkadian versions based on Hittite and Hurrian texts that go back to the second millennium B.C.[2]

The palace and library of Ashurbanipal were discovered by Hormuzd Rassam, who was assistant to the better-known archaeologist A. H. Layard in the excavation of Nineveh (1845–51). The twelve tablets of the Gilgamesh epic were part of an enormous collection of literary and historical documents. More than twenty thousand of the tablets were shipped to the British Museum. It was not until thirty years after Rassam's discovery that their full importance was realized. But the man who brought the attention of scholars to the significance of the Gilgamesh epic was George Smith, who deciphered the tablets in 1872. Among all the tablets sent by Rassam to the British Museum Smith found only fragments of the legend. He determined to find the rest of the pieces, and with the financial aid of the London Daily Telegraph *he went to Nineveh and finally succeeded in recovering the missing fragments. Upon his completion of the translation it became clear that this was the most important literary work ever to come from ancient Mesopotamia.*

The Gilgamesh epic is a kind of Sumerian Odyssey, *a dramatic account of the adventures of the hero who went* in search of the secret of immortality. "For the first time in the history of the world," writes E. A. Speiser, "a profound experience on such a heroic scale has found expression in a noble style. The scope and sweep of the epic and its sheer poetic power give it a timeless appeal." [3] The story as it finally appeared in twelve tablets represents a compilation of independent versions at first handed down by word of mouth and later written by different scribes. The twelfth tablet is an independent appendage to the previous material and is irrelevant to the main theme. In the twelfth tablet Gilgamesh calls upon the ghost of his friend Enkidu to inquire about the Hereafter. Enkidu's response is disillusioning and hopeless. The spirits of those who have passed on "find no rest in the nether-world."

The parallels between the Gilgamesh epic and the Hebrew flood story (Gen. 6, 7, 8) are numerous and similar enough to suggest dependence of the latter upon the former. In both the Sumerian and biblical accounts the hero is informed by divine revelation that the deluge is to occur. Both are alike in the description of the building of the ark, the embarkation, the cessation of rain, the resting of the ship on the mountain peak, the sending of the three birds, the disembarking, and the sacrifice. On the other hand, as with other literary parallels, the Sumerian account shows a more polytheistic and also less ethical point of view than the Hebrew.

All early civilizations seem to have had a flood legend. The Sumero-Akkadian story is known to have been based on actual occurrences. C. Leonard Woolley's excavations at Ur and Stephen Langdon's at Kish show a flood stratum at 4000 B.C. and a later one at 3300 B.C. These unprecedented inundations assumed great importance in the minds of the later Assyrians and Babylonians, thus accounting for the various recensions of the flood legend.

Gilgamesh, two-thirds god and one-third man, was a great hero and a warrior but he was also a tyrant. He built the walls of his city Uruk; he was unmatched in battle; he ruled with absolute power; and the people had to obey his slightest whim.

His arrogance and arbitrary domination over his people became intolerable, so they called upon the goddess Aruru to create "his double," a monster to match Gilgamesh in combat. "Let them do battle," they prayed, "and let the rival win so that Uruk may have peace."

Aruru answered their prayers and created Enkidu, a valiant god of battle, whose entire body was covered with hair, shaggy as a woman's head. His clothes were of animal skins and, like an animal, he grazed in the fields and fought with the wild beasts for a place at the water holes. It happened that a hunter laying traps for wild animals came upon him, and when he saw him he was terrified and ran to his village to report. He told his father of the creature who ranges over the hills, feeds with the beasts, and drinks at the watering place, who destroys all the traps and releases the animals. The father advised the hunter to go to Uruk and speak to Gilgamesh.

When Gilgamesh heard his story he told him to go back to his village, choose a harlot, and take her to the water hole, where, upon seeing Enkidu, she would remove her clothes and attract him. Once he had embraced her, the beasts would reject him, knowing that he was not one of them. In this way Enkidu would leave the wilderness to take up the ways of men. The hunter did as he was advised. He took the girl to the watering place and together they waited two days. On the third day the savage man came, whereupon the girl took off her garments and revealed her bosom. Enkidu immediately possessed her. She welcomed his ardor and for six nights they lay together. At length he arose and returned to the beasts. But on seeing Enkidu the wild beasts drew away from him and would have nothing to do with him. He tried to run but his legs became weak. He now knew that he was no longer one of the beasts but was a man.

Returning to the harlot, he sat at her feet and she said to him, "Thou art wise, Enkidu, and art become a god! Forsake this wild life and come with me to Uruk, where Gilgamesh lords it over the people." This pleased Enkidu and he replied, "Take me to the temple of Anu and Ishtar so that I can challenge Gilgamesh. I will show him that I am the one who is mighty!"

They arrived to find the city celebrating a holiday, and the young people, dressed in festive attire, were reveling in the streets. Then, surrounded by his retinue, Gilgamesh appeared. The procession stopped in the court of the temple. As Gilgamesh prepared to enter the temple, Enkidu stood in front of him and challenged him. The people gathered around the two warriors, noticing that they were evenly matched. Then the struggle began. They wrestled each other and the walls shook as they fought like snorting bulls. Gilgamesh at length was forced to the ground. Then he knew he had met his equal. Enkidu, for his part, recognized that Gilgamesh was not just an arrogant tyrant but a worthy opponent, and he said to him, "Let us be friends." They embraced each other and cast their lot together.

Gilgamesh then proposed that they go to the forest and cut down a cedar tree. But Enkidu replied that the keeper of the sacred forest was the mighty Humbaba, "whose mouth is fire and whose breath is death." Gilgamesh rebuked his companion, saying, "What about thy great might? Advance, fear not. It is better to fall fighting than not to have tried." So they had weapons made for them and set out for the forest. Both became fearful and began to regret their decision, and each had to encourage the other.

Finally they reached the edge of the sacred forest where Humbaba lived. It was the end of the day, and they were so fatigued that they lay down under a tree and immediately fell asleep. About midnight Gilgamesh awoke from a dream in which a mountain fell upon him but a giant rescued him. "This," said Enkidu, "is a portent of our victory over Humbaba." They arose and proceeded into the forest. Gilgamesh seized an axe and cut down a large cedar tree, which fell with such a crash that it aroused Humbaba. The monster rushed at them angrily, shouting, "Who had the temerity to fell the cedar in my forest?"

At this point Shamash, the sun god, spoke to Gilgamesh in reassurance and bade him go on. Shamash then sent a tempestuous wind against Humbaba, which blinded him. He was unable to move. Knowing that he was helpless he begged for mercy. "Let me go and I will be your servant." Enkidu and Gilgamesh did not listen to the giant's pleas but cut off his head.

Gilgamesh then washed himself and put on clean clothes, as well as a royal robe and crown. He looked so handsome that he attracted the attention of Ishtar, the goddess of womanhood. "Come with me," she said, "and be my husband. I shall give thee a chariot of gold. Kings and princes shall be at your service and bring you tribute. We shall live together in a beautiful palace." Gilgamesh replied: "Why should I take thee in marriage? You are but a fickle soul, a destroyer of men. You destroyed the god Tammuz, whom you condemned to hard labor and misery. So it was with thy father's gardener, who devoted himself to your comfort and delight. When he refused to lie with you, you turned him into a mole. There were many others whom you seduced and then ruined. It would be the same with me."

These insults made Ishtar fly to heaven to complain to Anu, her father, and Antum, her mother. But Anu replied that she had invited all this and deserved to be reminded of her foul deeds. The enraged Ishtar then demanded that Anu send the bull of heaven down to smite Gilgamesh; if he did not, she would smash the doors of the nether-world and release the dead, who would come to the earth and destroy the living. Anu said, "If I permitted that there would be seven years of famine on earth." But Ishtar said she was prepared for such an eventuality. So the bull came to the earth and plunged at Gilgamesh and Enkidu. Enkidu seized the bull by the horns and plunged a sword into the back of his neck. Then they tore his heart out and presented it to Shamash, the sun god.

Ishtar, having witnessed the conflict from the battle-ments of Uruk, cried, "Woe unto Gilgamesh who has slain the bull of heaven." Whereupon Enkidu, enraged that she credited the slaying to Gilgamesh alone, tore off the thigh of the bull and tossed it in her face. She then threatened Enkidu with terrible punishment. Ishtar pre-pared to give the bull a proper burial, but Gilgamesh gathered the remains of the bull and took them to Uruk to receive the tribute of the people.

Shortly after this incident Enkidu had a dream in which all the gods met in council to determine which of the two heroes was the more guilty of slaying the bull. Some said Gilgamesh was the more to blame and therefore must die. Others insisted it was Enkidu. After much wrangling over the question, Anu concluded, "Since Gilgamesh also cut down the sacred cedar, he is the one who must die." This only plunged the council into a greater dispute, as each member accused one hero or the other of being the cause of the slaying. Before they could come to a decision Enkidu awoke and told Gilgamesh about his dream.

Gilgamesh told his friend that he himself was equally guilty and that if Enkidu were put to death he would spend the rest of his life mourning his loss. Enkidu lay half awake reviewing his life and cursing the events that had led to this pass. Later he had another dream in which he was transformed into a monster and was carried to hell, to the house of lust inhabited by the queen of the netherworld. When he awoke he knew he was to die. He lay for twelve days stricken with grief and becoming weaker. Gilgamesh sat helpless beside him. At last he closed his eyes in death. Gilgamesh grieved bitterly at the loss of this friend, his right hand, the one who had fought and hunted with him. He paced back and forth wailing and pulling out his hair. He became afraid because he knew that he was destined to the same fate.

Having buried his friend, Gilgamesh then decided to go in search of Utnapishtim, who lived on the Mountain of Mashu and who reputedly held the secret of eternal life. After many days of travel he arrived at the mountain, whose peaks, it was said, "reach to heaven and whose breasts reach to the Netherworld." The gate to the mountain was guarded by a hideous scorpion-man who demanded of Gilgamesh the reason for his coming. Gilgamesh replied that he wanted to see Utnapishtim and learn the secret of immortality. "That," said the scorpion-man, "is impossible, for no mortal has ever reached the abode of Utnapishtim, which is approached by a dark tunnel twelve leagues long." Nevertheless, Gilgamesh was determined to go forward. The guard, perceiving that the traveler was two-thirds god, did not attempt to stop him but gave him his blessing.

The farther Gilgamesh walked the darker became the tunnel, until he could see nothing. But as he neared the end he saw light, and he soon found himself in a lush garden with trees bearing jewels. Shamash the sun god appeared to him and said, "Gilgamesh, rejoice, for thou art the first mortal to enter this paradise; but the life thou pursuest thou shalt not find." Heedless of the warning Gilgamesh pressed on until he came to a house. The custodian, an alewife, appeared and ordered the gate to be locked. At first she took Gilgamesh for a vagabond but on hearing his story she knew he was no ordinary fellow and bade him enter.

The alewife tried to discourage Gilgamesh and said, "The life thou pursuest thou wilt never find. When the gods created mankind, they determined that man should die. Therefore make the most of every day you have. Eat, dance, and make merry. Live the abundant life."

Gilgamesh was not deterred. He asked her how he could find Utnapishtim. The woman answered that he lived on a distant island across an ocean that no person had ever sailed. It was the Sea of Death. She told him, however, that Utnapishtim's boatman, Ursanabi, was in the house, having come on an errand, and perhaps he could take him across the ocean. She brought the boatman and he consented to do so. "But there is one stipulation," said the boatman: "You must avoid touching the waters of death. Once your pole has been dipped in the water, you must get rid of it and substitute another. Therefore you must go into the forest and cut down twice-sixty poles for the voyage."

This Gilgamesh did, and they boarded the boat. They sailed for a month and used up all the poles. Then Gilgamesh tore off his tunic and held it up as a sail. As they neared the island, Utnapishtim sat peering out over the ocean. Suddenly he spied the voyagers and said to himself, "Who are the men in the boat? Surely they are not my boatmen."

They disembarked and approached Utnapishtim. Gilgamesh related his story and then told him the object of his journey. Utnapishtim assured Gilgamesh that for man there is no such thing as eternal life. "Do we build a house forever? Do we seal contracts forever? The birds and flowers die sooner or later and so do mortal men. This has been decreed by the gods." To this Gilgamesh replied, "You yourself are a human being like me. Tell me, how do you enjoy the life of a god?"

The wise old man was silent for a while. Then he said: "I will reveal to you the secret that I share with the gods. Shurippak, a city on the Euphrates, was the home of the gods, who decided to bring about a great flood. Ea, god of the waters, warned me of the coming deluge and told me to build a ship. 'Give up your worldly goods and save thy life. Aboard the ship take seed of all living things.' I answered that I would carry out these orders, so I built the ship and sealed it with pitch. Ten dozen cubits was the height of each wall. I made six decks. I laid in supplies. Six measures of bitumen I poured into the furnace. Three measures of asphalt I poured inside. Oil was used for the caulking. I slaughtered sheep and bulls for meat and provided wine to drink. On the seventh day the ship was completed. I put in it what gold and silver I had. My family and kin I included. All beasts and birds filed into the ark.

"At dawn a dark cloud appeared and the thunder frightened even the gods. For seven days the boat was tossed about by the furious storm. On the seventh day the storm subsided and the flood ceased. All mankind had turned back into clay. I opened a hatch and saw the sunshine. The ship came to rest on Mount Nisir, which held it fast. For six days Mount Nisir held the ship fast. On the seventh day I sent forth a dove to see if it could find dry land upon which to light. The dove flew off but returned, having found no resting place. Then I sent forth a swallow but it also returned. Finally I sent forth a raven. The raven found a resting place, ate food, and did not come back. Thus I knew that the waters had diminished.

"We disembarked on the top of the mountain and offered sacrifices to the gods. The gods smelled the incense and gathered around the sacrificer. Then Enlil took me and my wife back aboard the ship, saying: 'Until this day Utnapishtim has been merely a mortal but henceforth he shall be as one of the gods. He shall reside forever on a faraway island at the mouth of the rivers.' "

His story finished, Utnapishtim told Gilgamesh that such a thing could not happen to him. Gilgamesh could not summon a meeting of the gods to grant him the favor of immortality. So he knew that his quest had been in vain. He slept for seven days and nights. When he awoke he asked Utnapishtim what he should do, for he had been warned in a dream that he was facing death. Utnapishtim called to Ursanabi the boatman and instructed him to get the boat ready. Turning to Gilgamesh he said, "I will disclose to you a secret. There is a plant at the bottom of the sea. It is like a buckthorn, and if you obtain this plant you will find new life."

Gilgamesh tied heavy stones to his feet and lowered himself. He found the plant and returned to the shore. "This famous plant," he said to the boatman, "will restore youth to the one who finds it. I will take it back to Uruk and call it 'Man Becomes Young in Old Age.' I shall eat it and become youthful again." They crossed the sea and began the journey by land to Uruk. They stopped at a well, where Gilgamesh bathed. While he was in the water a serpent snatched the plant and made off with it. Immediately the serpent cast off its skin and became young.

Gilgamesh sat down and wept. He realized again that he must face the fact of death like all mortals. He and Ursanabi walked home to Uruk.

The Mighty Works
of Marduk

〇〇〇〇〇〇〇〇〇〇〇〇〇〇〇〇〇〇

Rivaling the Gilgamesh epic in its importance as repre-
sentative religious literature of ancient Mesopotamia is the
Semitic creation epic that came to light in the British exca-
vations at Nineveh and was made available by George
Smith in 1876. It is an Akkadian epic, consisting of seven
tablets, from the second millennium B.C. *and is a copy of*
an earlier Sumerian tablet. The text upon which the ver-
sion in this book is based is made up of late copies from
the first millennium B.C.[4]

The story of the struggle between order and chaos was
a favorite one in all ancient cultures. In Mesopotamia it
was enacted as a play at the beginning of the New Year.

*As a spring pageant it included a celebration of the crea-
tion of the world and all life, the beginning of kingship
and world order. The protagonist of the drama is Marduk,
the supreme deity of Babylon, who vanquished Tiamat,
the dragon of the great deep or water deity, representing
the original chaos. Prior to the first Babylonian dynasty
(1900 B.C.) the Sumerian Enlil and Ea were supreme deities, but when the city of Babylon became the capital of
the Babylonian Empire, Marduk emerged as the chief Semitic god.*

*The first few lines of the epic recall the beginning of
Genesis: "In the beginning God created the heavens and
the earth. The earth was without form and void and darkness was upon the face of the deep."*

*There is less similarity between the Akkadian and Old
Testament creation stories than there is between the flood
stories from these two sources. The Genesis account of
the creation may be dependent to some extent on the older
Babylonian traditions, but the advanced religious genius
of the Hebrews produced a loftier and vastly more digni-
fied description of the event.*

*There is also a myth of the creation of man by the
mother goddess. This exists in an old Babylonian version
and is incomplete. According to E. A. Speiser, it was
probably shortened to be used as an incantation in connection with childbirth, "with the result that the myth itself seems to have been restated only in its bare outlines."*[5]

In the beginning there was no heaven and no earth. There
was nothing but water, which was ruled over by the gods
Apsu and Tiamat. No other gods existed. From these two

gods, in time, came two others, Lahmu and Lahamu; and then from them, Anshar and Kishar, who brought forth Anu, the god of heaven, and his son was Ea. Thus increased the divine family. They were a boisterous lot, quarreling and raising such a clamor that finally Apsu took action. Accompanied by his vizier he went to Tiamat and said, "I can stand this noise no longer. We must destroy these creatures. We must have peace and quiet." To this Tiamat did not agree. "We cannot do away with our own offspring." The vizier whispered into Apsu's ear, "Pay no attention to her. If you want peace and quiet you will have to get rid of these obstreperous troublemakers."

Apsu went to the gods and told them of his plans, whereupon they simply protested loudly and then became silent, brooding upon their fate. But Ea, the All-Wise, was not concerned. He had his own plan. Ea placed a spell on Apsu and the vizier, and soon they were sound asleep. Then, after tearing off Apsu's crown and robe and putting them on himself, Ea killed Apsu and took the vizier prisoner.

Ea and his wife, Damkina, celebrated the event by building a beautiful cottage. Here they lived, and to them was born Marduk, the mighty prince, the god of gods, king of kings, whose strength and wisdom made the heart of Ea rejoice. Marduk had four eyes and four ears, and fire came forth from his throat. He was taller, heavier, and stronger than any creature that had ever lived.

Now it was Marduk who enraged the gods with his pranks. So they went to Tiamat. "Remember your husband and how he was slain," they said. "Get up and put this Marduk in his place." She was finally persuaded and replied, "We shall take up the battle but first we shall have to get help."

A conference of the gods was held, and Tiamat created

eleven terrible monsters in whose veins ran poison instead of blood and whose claws were deadly. These horrible dragons were placed in the command of the god Kingu, who joined Tiamat in leading the forces to battle.

When Ea heard what had taken place he went to Anshar and told him. Anshar was quite partial to Marduk and, being his great-grandfather, had a warm spot in his heart for him. Anshar said to Ea, "You slew Apsu and took the vizier prisoner. Now you will have to put to death Tiamat and Kingu." Ea set out at once, but when he saw the terrible monsters coming toward him he turned and fled.

Anshar then turned to Anu and said, "My son, you must go to Tiamat. Beg her to desist from this course, but if she continues command her to obey my orders." But when Anu saw Tiamat and her forces he ran for his life. Now Anshar and his council were in despair, for it was clear that Tiamat intended to slay all the gods, not just the prankster Marduk. And none of the gods dared face Kingu and the terrible monsters.

Suddenly Ea thought of a plan. Marduk was the strongest creature who ever lived. What if he should become champion of the gods and fight Tiamat himself? If he won the other gods would be so grateful that they would forgive him for the trouble he had caused before. So he sent for Marduk, and advised him to visit his great-grandfather Anshar and volunteer to oppose Tiamat. But Marduk was crafty as well as strong. When he spoke to Anshar he placed one condition on his offer: he would have to be made king of all the gods and make all the decisions.

Anshar agreed and sent a messenger to Lahmu and Lahamu with instructions to call together a council of the gods. So they held a meeting of all the gods of heaven. Having heard the news of Tiamat's plans, they met at a banquet and elected Marduk chief of all deities and final arbiter in all things. He was placed upon a throne and given a sword and the symbols of kingship. Then the gods commended him to the task of overcoming Tiamat.

After the gods had dispersed Marduk prepared for the onslaught with bow and arrow and a net. He summoned the stormwinds to his side and set off in his chariot, which was drawn by four fierce dragons. When he arrived at the scene of battle, Kingu and his forces were thrown into confusion at the sight of him, but Tiamat stood her ground. Marduk rebuked her for defying the gods. He challenged Tiamat to battle to the death.

At this Tiamat flew into a rage and lunged at Marduk. He threw out his net, which closed about her and held her tight. He then called upon the stormwind, which blew so fiercely that it held her jaws open. Marduk shot an arrow into her open mouth. It went down her throat and penetrated her heart. She fell at Marduk's feet, dead. When they saw their leader die, Tiamat's forces attempted to flee, but they were taken prisoner and destroyed. Kingu was deprived of all authority and the eleven monsters were rendered powerless.

Then Marduk returned to Tiamat and smashed her skull. With one half of her corpse he made the firmament and the waters beneath. With the other half he formed the earth. He made Anu the god of heaven, Enlil the god of the air and earth, and Ea the god of the waters below. He stationed the other gods. He created the sun, the moon, and the constellations and set the stars in their courses; he determined the length of day and night, the week, the month, and the year.

When this was finished Marduk said to the gods, "I shall now make man and he shall serve the gods. I shall first make bone and blood with which to fashion him." But Ea said, "Why not make man out of the bones and blood of one of those who conspired against us?" This sounded reasonable to Marduk, who called the gods together to inquire who was the chief offender. They shouted, "Kingu was the ringleader, let him be sacrificed!"

Kingu was brought forth; his head was cut off, and from his blood and bones was formed a man. Then the gods praised Marduk the Creator and built for him a city—Babylon—and in it a great shrine where he would live and to which they would come to pay him homage. From this royal abode Marduk ruled the world in wisdom. And each year on New Year's Day he was worshipped in the celebration of the renewal of life.

Adapa at the Gate of Heaven

The story of Adapa exists in four fragments, one of which was found at Amarna in Egypt and the others in the library of Ashurbanipal at Nineveh. The texts date from the fourteenth and the seventh centuries B.C., respectively.[6] The protagonist of the myth is the wise Adapa, sage of Eridu.

The story is usually interpreted as referring to man's lost opportunity to achieve immortality. (Adapa is equated with the generic word for "man" and also the person "Adam.") Adapa became too ambitious and Ea, his creator, jealous of his achievements and fearful that he would attain too much knowledge, caused him to be thrust from

42

*the gates of heaven to live the precarious life of an ordi-
nary mortal.*

*It has also been the custom to draw an analogy between
the Adapa myth and the Adam story in the Old Testament (Gen. 3) and to see the latter as derived from the
former. The connection becomes somewhat plausible in
view of the serpent theme pictured on early Sumerian
bowls. One typical rendering of the theme shows a snake
guarding the tree of life. On another the serpent stands
behind a woman. A third shows a man and a woman seated;
between them stands the tree of life, and behind the woman
is a serpent.⁷ This points to the existence of a Sumerian
legend connecting the serpent with vegetation and serving
as a tempter of the woman. The Hebrew legend of the
eating of the forbidden tree of knowledge and its implica-
tion of the origin of sin is thought to have come from
the Adapa myth.⁸ Of course, the biblical story contains elements not found in the Babylonian, but the themes of
paradise, the deception by the god or the serpent, and the
expulsion are present in both. In one Sumerian account
man is placed in a garden and "forbidden to eat of the
tree of knowledge of good and evil." In Genesis Adam is
also commanded not to eat from the tree that would give
him a knowledge of evil. Into this scene comes the serpent
to deceive Adam and Eve by promising them the secrets
of heaven if they eat the fruit. Eve does eat, and gives
fruit to her husband, and they became conscious of evil.
Mortality and pain henceforth become the lot of mankind.
This legend seems to have had its origin in the Sumerian
accounts. The motif of the perverted message—man for-
feiting immortality because a divine message telling him
how to attain it is misrepresented by the messenger—was
a common one in the ancient world and forms the basis of
the Old Testament story.⁹*

This generally accepted interpretation of the Adapa

*myth has recently been questioned. Theodor H. Gaster
claims that Adapa is not a human being, so that the theme
of the story is not—as has been generally thought—
"man's loss of immortality." According to Gaster, Adapa
is a "special kind of creature, fashioned as a prank by the
god Ea—neither man nor god, but something betwixt and
between, possessing the form of the one and the intelligence of the other." [10] Only on this basis, he explains, can
we understand how Adapa is powerful enough to break
the wings of the wind. But beyond this slight variation
there is little difference between Gaster's view and that of
other Sumerologists. Ea's deceitful advice to Adapa is
given because he does not want his protégé to become a
full-fledged god. When Adapa follows this advice, it is
clear that he is a mortal after all. However, he is something more than man, and after his return to earth Anu
makes him immune to all the ills of human beings.*

Ea created Adapa, a creature who looked like a man but
had the wisdom of a god. There was little that Adapa did
not know or could not do. He could fish, hunt, and bake
as well as anyone. He provided the city of Eridu with food
and drink and saw to the safety of the people. He was
pious as well as clever and observed all the laws of the
land and the priestly rites.

One day when Adapa was fishing a fierce storm came
up and the South Wind in the form of a gigantic bird
tossed the boat about in the waves. Finally a heavy gust
overturned the craft and Adapa floundered about in the
sea. Infuriated, he cursed the South Wind and caused its
wings to be broken.

For seven days the wind failed to blow and the sea was calm. This troubled the god Anu, who called upon his vizier to investigate. The vizier told him what had happened. Anu was angry and commanded Adapa to be brought before him. At this point Ea, the all-wise god of Eridu, intervened, advising Adapa as follows:

"You must wear your hair long and untidy, put ashes on your head, and dress in mourning. There will be two guards standing before the gate of heaven—Tammuz and Gishzida, two gods who once lived on earth. When they see you they will ask you why you are in mourning. You will answer that you mourn the disappearance of two gods from the earth. When they ask you who these two gods are you will answer that they are Tammuz and Gishzida. This will please them and cause them to intercede for you before Anu. There is one more thing: when you stand before the judge of heaven you will be offered food and drink, but you must not take it for it is the food and drink of death."

Then a messenger arrived, charging Adapa with breaking the wings of the South Wind and summoning him to the court of heaven. Here Anu demanded an explanation of Adapa's action. Adapa told the god what had happened on the sea. Anu was perplexed and undecided. Tammuz and Gishzida, flattered by Adapa's mourning for them, interceded in his behalf. They told Anu that he was a righteous man and faithful to the gods and that he did not deserve punishment. Anu was impressed by their defense and said, "Adapa is not guilty and shall be freed. Ea has given him godlike powers, but since he is still mortal let us grant him the status of a god and give him the food and drink of eternal life."

Adapa followed Ea's advice and refused the food and drink, thinking it was the food and drink of death. Then Anu said, "It seems that Adapa prefers to remain a mere mortal and refuses the food and drink of immortality. Send him back to earth to toil as a man and to be a victim of man's ailments and weaknesses." But on second thought Anu relented and, thinking of Adapa's piety and honesty, said, "Adapa, you must go back to earth but you will not be subject to the diseases and misfortunes of man. The goddess Ninkarrak will protect you from all ills. When sickness, disaster, or misfortune comes, Ninkarrak will turn it aside. You will be king of Eridu and your heirs will be kings."

So Adapa was deprived of eternal life but lived like a god in this life.

Innana's Descent into Hell

A number of Sumerian myths concern Innana—the Akka-dian Ishtar, queen of heaven and goddess of love—and her husband Dumuzi, the biblical Tammuz. The story of In-nana's descent to the netherworld has come down to us in Sumerian and Akkadian versions. The Semitic or Akka-dian story exists in several recensions, coming from Ashur and Nineveh. Hitherto unknown fragments from 1750 B.C. have recently come to light and have been edited, thus necessitating new translations. The complete English text has been prepared from the additional tablets by Samuel N. Kramer.[11]

Innana, the queen of heaven, decided to go to the underworld, the land of no return, the land of darkness and
dust. Her purpose in going was to reign there in place of
her sister Ereshkigal. Arriving at the entrance she called
to the watchman, "Open the gates or I will break them
down and will cause the dead to rise and the living to die."
The gatekeeper replied, "Spare the doors; I will go to the
queen and tell her of your arrival." He did so and Ereshkigal was enraged that her sister had come to her realm.
"What have I done that she should come here to interfere?
But go and receive her with the customary procedure."

The gatekeeper returned to the entrance and admitted
Innana. As she entered the first door he took her crown
from her head. She asked him why this was done and he
replied that that was one of the rules laid down by the
queen of the netherworld. When she entered the second
gate, he deprived her of her earrings. At the third door he
took her necklace; at the fourth, the jewelry adorning her
breasts; at the fifth, her waistband; at the sixth, her ankle
and wrist clasps; and at the seventh, her clothes.

Immediately upon Innana's entrance through the final
door Ereshkigal condemned her for entering her realm
and said to her vizier, "Imprison her in the palace and
afflict her with the sixty maladies—the diseases of the eyes,
ears, hands, feet, heart, stomach, and head." So Innana
suffered the torments of the damned and was left to die.

On the earth, after Innana had left for the underworld,
the animals no longer mated and men no longer lay with
women. Papsukkal, messenger of the gods, was over-
whelmed with grief and clothed himself in the garments of
mourning. He informed Ea of Innana's descent to the

netherworld and its consequences on the earth. In response
Ea created Asusunamir, a eunuch and very beautiful, and
sent him to Ereshkigal so that, being pleased with his appearance, she might release Innana at his request. Ea said
to Asusunamir, "After Ereshkigal has seen you and has
become calm you must ask her for the water of life that
you might drink it." Asusunamir followed Ea's instructions but Ereshkigal replied, "Asusunamir, you have requested something that is impossible. I curse you with a
great curse. Your bread will be the bread from the street
and your drink will be that of the sewer. You shall have no
dwelling place except with the drunkards." So Asusunamir
became the substitute for Innana in the underworld.
Ereshkigal then commanded that Innana be given the
water of life and conducted through the seven gates to the
upper world. As she passed through each gate Namtar,
the vizier, returned her garments and jewels.

THE
MYTHS
AND TALES
OF ANCIENT EGYPT

EGYPTIAN PANTHEON

The Great Ennead

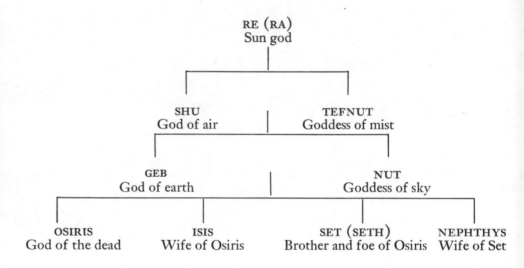

RE (RA)
Sun god

SHU
God of air

TEFNUT
Goddess of mist

GEB
God of earth

NUT
Goddess of sky

OSIRIS
God of the dead

ISIS
Wife of Osiris

SET (SETH)
Brother and foe of Osiris

NEPHTHYS
Wife of Set

NOTE

*Unlike the other pantheon charts in this book, the
levels of the Egyptian pantheon show generations of
descent, from Re, the sun god. A lesser Ennead consists of Thoth, god of writing; Anubis, god of em-
balming; Horus, son of Osiris; and others.*

The Paradox of Egypt

In the period around 3000 B.C., by which time the Egyptian civilization was in full bloom, writing had been invented and the two lands of Upper and Lower Egypt had been united. These two factors are profoundly significant, for they made possible the documentary recording of history from that time on and the political unity of the whole territory from the Delta to the Sudan. In that same period the calendar of 365 days, 12 months, and 24 hours to the day was established; the potter's wheel was invented; and stone masonry was used. There was developed a style of artistic expression that was more enduring than that of any

53

other people in history—a style which in portrait sculpture, relief, architecture, and calligraphy lasted for more than three millennia. Here, two thousand years before Athens, Imhotep perfected the basic forms of architecture: fluted columns with astragal bases and flowered capitals, wall niches and projections, portals, ornamented friezes, and pillared halls. Painted pottery in four colors and tomb paintings told the story of Egyptian life and afterlife. Medical and legal literature existed as early as 2700 B.C.

These accomplishments indicate that the Egyptians of 3000–2500 B.C. were far from primitive in their mentality. To formulate surgical methods without recourse to magic or to construct pyramids with nothing but the ramp, the lever, and some copper tools means that reason, sophistication, and creative genius were present and that there was probably less magic and superstition in 3000 B.C. than two millennia later. This presents an apparent paradox as far as mythology is concerned, for we have elsewhere defined myth as the science of primitive man, the superstition of the untrained mind. The answer can only be that the early Egyptian used reason where necessary but in spiritual and cosmic matters beyond his comprehension resorted to myth and symbol.

The basic belief of the ancient Egyptians, the conviction around which all else grew, was the changelessness of the universe. Everything in their environment pointed to the one fact that the world was static, and with that observation went a further conviction that changelessness was the only real and unchangeable truth. The modern idea of evolution, flux, and variation had no place in the Egyptians' world view. Their profound sense of cosmic order seemingly ruled out variety of interpretation. Their language, art, and architecture, for instance, remained fundamentally the same for three millennia. Here we have another apparent inconsistency in the fact that for each mythological subject there were many different concepts and interpretations existing side by side. The same held true for religious ideas and theology in general. In the early period there was a great tolerance of belief, with no rigid doctrine to be uniformly adhered to. Exception to this came in the Amarna period (fourteenth century B.C.). Furthermore, the same priest or scribe could subscribe to various and contradictory ideas of the same subject, e.g., a god, sky, creation. Also we find that frequently one deity or sacred object was identified or equated with another. So change and diversity appeared in the mythological field as contrasted to the general philosophy of changelessness and permanence.

From another point of view the myth with its diversity of interpretation might be considered to support the idea of permanence. By connecting the ephemeral and transitory events of this life to the changeless and eternal reality of the divine world, the realm of the gods, the myth reduced the fears and uncertainties of human life. It presented the daily events of humanity as small particles of the cosmic order, and this made for faith. The Pharaoh was not just a mortal but a god and the embodiment of *Maat*.[1] The myths of Egypt made this connection between the human and the divine, and it was reassuring to the common man.[2]

A final apparent paradox lies in the coexistence of the myth with the basic pragmatism of the Egyptians. The Egyptians were nothing if not practical. Their literature shows little ability in the field of speculative thought or abstract ideas. Their cosmology, their beliefs about the afterlife, and their religious and ethical teachings are expressed in terms of the physical and the tangible, the practical necessities of daily life. The genius of the Egyptians was not in theorizing or inventiveness but in their astounding accomplishments with what they had at their disposal and in their capacity for organization and administration. This attitude would tend to exclude the mystical and the mysterious in life, but as was stated before, the Egyptians resorted to symbol and legend to make comprehensible the events and figures of the nonsensuous, unknown world. Consequently, every god and every otherworldly event was conceived through a symbol, a tale, or a ritual. Sometimes, as in the case of the Osiris-Horus myth, they used both tale and ritual, the funeral rites in this case illustrating the myth.

The purpose of the tale or legend was either to explain a cosmic event or person or merely to entertain. By the latter part of the third millennium B.C. the important mythological concepts in Egypt were firmly established, some having been inherited from prehistory. By 2300–2000 B.C. the Pyramid Texts had been inscribed on the walls of the pyramids and the Coffin Texts were in use. These were the two chief nuclei of Egyptian mythology, the former containing funeral rites and the latter, requirements for admission into the afterlife.

The Egyptian Pantheon

Egyptian religion goes back into prehistoric times, when people regarded the sky, the heavenly bodies, and the processes of nature with reverence. They also stood in awe of animals; in fact, their first deities were represented in animal form. As religious thought developed in the historic period, many gods were portrayed as human beings with animal heads. Anubis, the god of the dead, was pictured as a jackal, whose function was to watch over the tombs. He also presided over the weighing of the heart of the deceased at the judgment hall of Osiris. Thoth, the god of wisdom and learning and the official scribe of

57

the afterworld, was alternately shown as an ibis and a baboon. As a scribe he is seen in the typical Egyptian judgment scene recording the results of the balancing of the heart and feather. As a local deity Thoth was worshipped at Hermopolis, where a live ibis was kept in the temple. He was associated also with the moon, which overcame the darkness with his light.

Khnum, the deity of Elephantine (an island in the Nile at Aswan), was associated with the myths of creation and was portrayed as a ram. He was supposed to have created each individual from clay. Sobek, the crocodile god, seems to have ruled originally over the Fayum and was the god of its capital, Crocodilopolis. Here live reptiles and crocodiles were kept in pools. Sobek was also identified with Re, the solar deity, and in some localities with Osiris. As water god, he symbolized the annual flooding of the Nile and its fertilization of the valley.

Among all the manifestations of nature the most prominent object of worship was the sun, a logical consequence of the feeling of dependence upon it. Much of the Egyptian ideology revolved about the sun and the river.[3] The chief sun deity was Re, the god of Heliopolis, who became a national god in the Fifth Dynasty (2750–2625 B.C.) and the most important deity in the pantheon. As the sun disk, Re had been regarded as a god since the Second Dynasty, three hundred years before. He was merged with local deities—Amon-Re, Khnum-Re, and Sobek-Re—thus enabling priests to maintain their local worship along with the state worship. Re was represented as a hawk-headed man but was also symbolized by the beetle or Khepri, rolling its ball of dung across the sky to depict the sun in its daily course. In this sense Re was regarded as the lord of creation.[4]

One of the major female deities was Hathor, who had a

human body and the head of a cow or a human head with a pair of cow's horns. She figures prominently in many myths as the goddess of love, beauty, and childbirth and is pictured both as a cruel deity and a gentle nurse, the Golden One. She wore the sun disk between her horns and may be regarded therefore as a solar deity.

Ptah is an example of a god in fully human form. He was the god of craftsmen and came into being as the ruling deity of Memphis, the capital of the Old Kingdom.

Amon appeared comparatively late in Egyptian history. He was the god of Thebes when that city became the capital of Egypt and when the Middle Kingdom was founded. Because of the prominence of Thebes in the Middle and New kingdoms Amon acquired more than local status. He was identified with Re and was represented as a crowned king with the sun's rays emanating from his head. Otherwise his crown was in the form of two feathers, which stood for Upper and Lower Egypt. The priests of Amon became the most powerful group in all Egypt, and the Amon temple complex at Thebes was the most colossal in history. Amon, king of the gods, succeeded Re as god of the universe, and his worship extended to Nubia, Syria, and Palestine.

There was an interlude in the polytheistic history of Egypt when Ikhnaton (reigned 1375–1358 B.C.) established the new monotheistic cult of Atonism, the worship of the solar disk. Opposing the Amon priesthood, this ruler, shortly after his accession to the throne, changed his name from Amenhotep IV to Ikhnaton (Akhenaton) and built a new capital at Akhet-Aton (the modern Tell el-Amarna), where he and his followers worshipped Aton. His complete neglect of politics and disregard for the deterioration of the empire caused his downfall, whereupon the military and the Amon priesthood resumed con-

trol of Egypt. His successor, Tutankhaton, upon returning to the former capital of Thebes, reverted to Amon
worship and changed his name back to Tutankhamon.

After the Amarna heresy, in which Aton was the sole
deity, Amonism became stronger than ever and even took
on a more spiritual and less anthropomorphic character.
It retained some of the aspects of Ikhnaton's monotheism:
Amon-Re was symbolized by the sun's rays and was regarded as creator and lord of all life and light. Although
Amonism itself contained a hint of monotheism, the poly-
theism of Egyptian religion in general was in no way modi-
fied.

It remains for us to identify the members of the Great
Ennead or family of the gods.[5] This grouping represents
the lineage of Horus, the falcon god. A basic concept of
the Egyptian culture was that the pharaoh was both god
and king. As god-king he was the embodiment of both the
heavenly world and the state. This idea started with Horus,
who was identified with the king of Egypt as early as the
First and Second dynasties (3400–2980 B.C.). Horus was
known as the Lord of Heaven and the ruler of all Egypt.
With the unification of Egypt the trinitarian concept of
Horus as king of heaven, king of the earth, and sacred
falcon became an established feature of the Egyptian religion. The idea of the universality and eternal existence of
Horus also goes back to the First Dynasty and is found
in the Pyramid Texts.[6]

The most illustrious deity of the Ennead was Osiris,
who was supposed to have ruled on earth as king. After
being put to death by Seth, Osiris became god of the dead.
He was identified with the Nile and its annual overflow
and thus was called the god both of reviving vegetation
and of resurrection of the dead. The Osirian cult became
the dominant influence in the Egyptian religion. Perhaps

the most familiar subject from Egyptian art is the judgment scene in which the heart of the deceased is weighed
against the feather of truth. If they balance, and the deeds
of the deceased have been worthy, he is taken to Osiris,
who grants him immortality.

Isis, wife and sister of Osiris and mother of Horus, was
the goddess of love and the counterpart of Ishtar, Asherah,
Astarte, Cybele, Aphrodite, and Venus. Isis as the Great
Mother and faithful wife, became the most popular of all
female deities. The cult of the mother goddess continued
among the Greeks and the Romans and even found expression in the Mariolatry of Christianity.

In the Egyptian account of creation it was explained
that Shu was the god of the air and it was his function to
support the weight of heaven. Tefnut was the consort of
Shu and the goddess of moisture. From Shu and Tefnut
came Geb, the god of the earth, and Nut, the goddess of
the sky. As sky goddess, Nut gave birth each morning
to the sun and each evening to the stars. She was pictured
arched over the earth with hands and feet touching the
ground and with sun, moon, and stars in her body. She
was called "the Great Lady who gave birth to the gods,
the Mistress of the Two Lands."

From Geb and Nut came Osiris, Isis, Seth, and Nephthys. Seth, brother and foe of Osiris and enemy of
Horus, was thought of as a devil opposed to the good,
but also as a good god who fought on the side of Re. He
was regarded as Lord of Upper Egypt and was associated
with the desert and storms. Nephthys, sister of Isis, was
the goddess of women and was usually pictured with Isis
in the judgment hall of Osiris.

The Legend of Creation

The Egyptians gave much thought to the afterlife but they seemed to be less concerned about the origin of life. The written material on the subject of creation, in fact, is by comparison very meager. According to Egyptian mythology life evolved from the primeval waters. The creator Atum, whose name is interchangeable with Re and Khepri, rose from the waters of chaos and made a mound of dry earth, upon which he stood. The "primeval hillock" from which the first life came was supposedly located at Hermopolis, home of the sun god, although the same distinction was claimed for other sacred sites. (Typical of all cosmogonic events and personalities in Egypt, the creation story had several versions and all were accepted.) It is easy to recognize the source of this idea in the emerging of the first mound of mud from the receding waters of the flooded Nile. That bit of moist, fertilized silt, rising into the warm sunlight, would logically suggest the birthplace of new life. There may be some connection between the idea of the primeval hill as the place of creation or new life and the "high place" in all ancient Near Eastern countries (ziggurat, pyramid, local shrine, or temple).

The first account of the origin of life, from a Middle Kingdom version of the Book of the Dead, tells of the creation by Atum with his first appearance on the primeval hill. There is little analogy to the Genesis story, the only similarity being the creation arising from the waters or formless chaos. Another version also describes the creation by Atum. The text of this account was inscribed on the walls of two twenty-fourth-century pyramids. Still another version, appearing on a papyrus of 300 B.C. but undoubtedly retaining the content of a document from 2000 B.C., was created for ritualistic purposes and connects the creation with the daily repulsing of the dragon Apophis, who endangered the nightly voyage of Re's ship through the underworld. The text, Papyrus Bremner-Rhind, probably originated in Thebes. It is now in the British Museum.[7] The story of the creation occupies the last section of the papyrus, which is called The Book of Overthrowing Apophis, the Enemy of Re, and the Enemy of Osiris.

I am Atum, who appeared alone on the primeval hill, rising from the waters of chaos. When I appeared, heaven had not come into being; neither had the earth, nor the creatures of the earth. I lifted myself up from the water and made a foundation upon which to stand. Then I made every form to come from my mouth. First I made Shu and Tefnut by spewing them from my mouth. They became gods with me.

My eye followed after them as I observed them through the long periods of time. Finally they returned and restored my eye. I shed tears and men were made from the tears. After my eye returned it was angry with me because I had made another one in its place.

I arose from the plants and created reptiles and all creeping things. Shu and Tefnut gave birth to Geb and Nut. Geb and Nut brought forth Osiris, Horus, Seth, Isis, and Nephthys. From them came forth many children to multiply the earth.

These gods were sent forth to destroy Apophis, my archenemy who is no more. I put a curse upon him and all his children. The enemy of Re is consumed. Re shall drive across the heavens in peace. Life! Prosperity! Health!

The Feud Between
Horus and Seth

One of the most popular tales in the taverns of ancient Thebes was one called "The Contendings of Horus and Seth." It is hard, perhaps, to imagine the Egyptians telling humorous stories about their gods in the manner of the later Greeks with their ribald satires. But the Egyptians were no less sophisticated, and their literature contains much satirical fiction in which the divinities betray all the weaknesses of human beings. The "Contendings" is the best example of this form of myth.

The story is concerned with the contest of Horus and Seth for the rule of Egypt. The dramatis personae *are al-*

most all the chief deities in the Egyptian pantheon, and the tale itself is a clever lampoon of political bureaucracy and red tape that has a certain relevance for the modern reader. It represents a long accumulation of mythical episodes, all of which are deeply rooted in Egyptian tradition. Needless to say, the indignities attributed to the gods throughout the tale in no way detracted from the fanatical reverence paid to these gods by the same people who enjoyed the satire. In true mythical style, the "Contendings" contains many contradictions and inconsistencies, both in plot and in character. The sun god, as we have previously mentioned, often assumed both different names and different forms. This tendency was due to the Egyptians' desire to retain and combine everything, especially names and forms of deities—a tendency seen in the recognition of the two lands Upper and Lower Egypt. They were distinct and yet one. In the "Contendings" this combining tendency is illustrated by Isis' promise to Re-Atum that she will make an appeal to Atum of Heliopolis and Khepri, who are both the same god. Similarly Onuris is used for Shu, the god of air who separates heaven and earth. Neith, the goddess of Saïs in the Delta, was associated with Isis and Hathor and shared the same attributes.

The text is from Thebes and was written in the twelfth century B.C. in hieratic, a simplified cursive form of hieroglyphic writing. It is called the Chester Beatty Papyrus and was edited and translated by Alan H. Gardiner.[8]

This is the record of the judging of Horus and Seth, mightiest of princes who ever lived. It took place before

Re-Atum, the Master of the Universe. Horus laid claim to the office of king because he was the son of Osiris, god of the netherworld.

Shu arose and said, "All justice is powerful. Give the kingly office to Horus."

"That is only just and right," cried Thoth, the Scribe, to the Ennead.

Then Isis approached North Wind and said, "Let us send the good news to Osiris in the netherworld." At this Re-Atum was very angry, for he wanted to give the kingly office to Seth.

"What are we to do?" cried Onuris, to which Re-Atum replied, "Let us refrain from hasty action but send a letter to Neith and abide by her decision."

So the Ennead dictated to Thoth a letter to Neith, the Mighty: "Life! Health! Strength! I am writing to ask you what we should do about these two men, Horus and Seth, who have been contending for eighty years for the kingship. Nobody knows how to decide the matter. Will you give us your decision?"

Neith replied: "Award the office of Osiris to his son Horus, else I shall be angry and cause the heavens to crash to the ground. Also I advise Re-Atum to double the possessions of Seth and give him his two daughters, Anat and Astarte."

Thoth read the letter to Re-Atum and the Ennead. The latter agreed wholeheartedly, but Re-Atum was angry with Horus and said, "Horus, you are not fit for this high office." At this Onuris and all the gods of the Ennead were provoked and one of them insulted Re-Atum, who cast himself to the floor and lay there on his back for the rest of the day while the Ennead left the hall.

The next day the court reconvened and Re-Atum said to Horus and Seth, "Speak for yourselves."

Seth replied, "I am the strongest of all gods. I slay the enemy of Re-Atum daily. I am entitled to the office of Osiris." The Ennead all agreed. "Seth is right," they said.

"This is not right," said Horus. "It is unjust that I should be deprived of the office of my father in the presence of the Ennead." He was supported by Isis, who became angry with the Ennead; she vowed that these proceedings would be placed before Khepri and that the Ennead would be punished.

Sensing danger because of the testimony of Isis, Seth swore before the Master of the Universe, "I will not be a part of this hearing while Isis is in it." At this Re-Atum replied, "Well then, let us cross over to the Island-in-the-Midst and the Ennead will judge between them there. And instruct the ferryman not to ferry across any woman." The Ennead then crossed over to the island.

Presently Isis approached the ferryman, who was waiting by his boat. She had disguised herself as an old woman, bent over and haggard, and had a gold ring on her finger.

"I would like to be ferried across to the island," she said. "I have this jar of flour for a little boy who has been tending cattle for a week and he is hungry."

"I have been told," said the ferryman, "not to ferry across any woman."

"Was that on account of Isis?" she queried.

The ferryman asked in turn, "What will you give me to take you over?"

"I will give you this loaf," said Isis.

"I have been told not to ferry across any woman; it is hardly worth the risk for a mere loaf of bread."

"I will give you this ring," she said.

"Let me have it," the ferryman replied. She gave it to him and he rowed her across to the island.

As Isis walked along, she saw the Ennead and the Master of the Universe in his arbor. Seth saw her coming from a distance, whereupon she changed herself into a beautiful maiden. He immediately fell in love with her and overtook her in the woods.

He called to her and she said, "I was the wife of a herdsman and I bore him a male child. After my husband died my son tended the cattle. Then a foreigner came to my son and threatened to beat him, take away the cattle, and cast him out. I wish that you act in defense of my son."

Seth said, "The cattle should not be given to a stranger while the son is still alive."

Isis transformed herself into a kite and flew off to the top of an acacia tree. "Weep for yourself," she called to Seth. "You have judged yourself guilty and undeserving of the office." Then Seth went to Re-Atum and told him that Isis had deceived him into accusing himself with his own mouth. Re-Atum admitted that Seth had judged himself. The ferryman was summoned, and they forced him to confess that he was a disgrace to his own city.

The Ennead returned to the judgment hall, where Seth challenged Horus to a test. They would both become hippopotami and dive into the water. Whoever survived beneath the water for three months would receive the office. They plunged into the water. Isis was frightened and made a harpoon with which she speared Seth. When he begged her to withdraw the barb she had compassion and did so. This made Horus angry at his mother and he chopped off her head.

Re-Atum sent Seth in search of Horus to punish him. He found him lying under a tree and, throwing him on his back, cut out both his eyes, which he buried in the earth. Seth returned to Re-Atum and reported, "I did not find Horus." But Lady Hathor found Horus weeping. She poured the milk of the gazelle into his eyes and they were restored.

This made Seth all the more angry, and he challenged

Horus to a boat race, saying, "Each will build a ship of stone and whoever prevails over the other will be given the office of kingship." Horus built a ship of cedar and plastered it with gypsum. When it was lying on the water, Seth saw it and thought it was made of stone. So he cut off a mountain peak and made a great ship of stone. Then in the presence of the Ennead the two contenders took to their ships. Seth's ship sank immediately, and Seth changed himself into a hippopotamus and caused Horus' ship to sink.

At this, Horus wanted to cast a spear at Seth, but the Ennead warned him against that. Thoth suggested sending a letter to Osiris, asking for his judgment. Shu joined in, "That's the thing to do."

So the letter was written to Osiris, who replied to Re-Atum, "Why would you keep the office of kingship from my son since the gods and all those who came later owe their existence to me? I made the barley which they eat."

Re-Atum replied thus: "Suppose you had never been born. Some other god would have made the barley."

"It is true, you have done well in your way," replied Osiris. "You created the Ennead. But consider the responsibility and power I have. Whoever does evil I will send for to be judged here in the netherworld before me. Did not Ptah tell the stars and all creation to go to the netherworld where King Osiris is and take their rest?"

When this letter was read to the court the Ennead agreed, "He is right, right in every way."

Then it was that Horus was awarded the office. Re-Atum ordered that Seth be brought in handcuffs before him. "Why did you try to take this office instead of abiding by our judgment?" asked Re-Atum. Seth, who meanwhile had become reconciled to the situation, answered, "Let Horus come and be given the office."

Horus was brought, a crown was placed upon his head, and he was proclaimed king. "Life! Prosperity! Health! You are the king of Egypt." Even his mother Isis, who had been restored to life, was glad that he was king. "You are the good king," she cried. "My heart rejoices that you enlighten the earth with your presence."

Thereupon Re-Atum said, "Let Seth be given to me and be as my son. He shall thunder in the sky and men shall fear him."

This pleased everybody. Re-Atum said, "Be joyful. To the ground before Horus, son of Isis."

Isis joined in the festivities: "Horus has arisen as ruler. The Ennead is in holiday and heaven is in joy. Life! Prosperity! Health!"

The Tale of Sinuhe

This tale of an expatriate and his love for his own country became one of the most popular stories in ancient Egypt, testimony to which is seen in the number of extant manuscripts containing it. It was written by a poet who cared more for style than for plot, his literary ability being evident in his power of selection, his humor, and his use of unusual idioms, all of which must have attracted the ancient Egyptians.

The story of Sinuhe has retained its popularity to the present day, and its appeal has never ceased to intrigue the modern reader. It served as the inspiration for Mika

Waltari's The Egyptian, *which has been translated into ten languages. Recent studies have shown that the story was written in the Middle Kingdom. In spite of the current vogue of the non-novel and the plotless work of fiction, romantic stories of adventure will always have their appeal. For this reason the tale of Sinuhe has been included in this collection.*

The story may be largely fiction, but it is difficult to escape the impression that it is based on facts. Geographically and chronologically, the details as well as the main outline bear the marks of historicity. Sir Flinders Petrie preferred to regard the whole story as strictly historical, a biographical inscription of the early tombs: "Probably some day the tomb of Sinuhe may be found, and the whole inscription be read upon the walls."[9]

The story opens in the year 1960 B.C., when a messenger brought word to the co-regent Sesostris I, who was returning from a campaign against the Lybians, that Amenemhet I had died. Sesostris returned secretly to Thebes to entrench himself as pharaoh before any rival could take action, while Sinuhe, who had overheard the messenger give the news to Sesostris, fled from Egypt, perhaps for political reasons. The titles given to Sinuhe at the opening are those of high rank and show that he was a son of the king or of a noble of some importance. And his reception upon returning to Thebes confirms the supposition. The land to which Sinuhe fled seems to have been Edom or the southeast corner of Syria, a fertile and prosperous country. Aside from any other consideration, the story provides valuable information about the interior of Palestine and Syria in the time of Abraham.[10]

The hereditary prince, the royal seal-bearer, the administrator of foreign lands, beloved confidant of the king,
Sinuhe, tells the following story:

"I was the king's henchman and a servant of the king's
harem, waiting on the royal wife, the royal consort of
Sesostris.

"In the thirtieth year, on the ninth day of the third
month, the god-king entered his horizon. King Amenemhet
flew away to heaven and was united with the sun. He was
united with his creator. The palace was silenced and in
mourning; the gates were closed and the people grieved.

"Now His Majesty had dispatched an army to the land
of the Temehu with his son Sesostris as leader. He was
now returning with captives and cattle. Messengers from
Thebes met us on the road and informed Sesostris, who
departed for the capital immediately without telling the
army of the matter. I was standing nearby and overheard
the message.

"I trembled at the news and felt faint. Then I sought a
place to hide. I set out for the south off the beaten track
and traveled all night. In the morning I met a man who
was afraid of me and asked for mercy. By evening I was
near Kher-ahau. Here I crossed the river on a raft and
came to the quarries of Aku, the region of the Mistress of
the Red Mountain. After resting a few hours I pressed on
to the north until I reached the walls of the fort that was
built to repel the Bedouins. I hid in the bushes lest the
men on watch spy me. I hurried on and came to Peten
and the Island of Kemwer. I suffered from thirst and said
to myself, 'This is the taste of death.' I screwed up my
courage and rose to continue when I saw several Bedouins,

Terra-cotta female figurine from Tepe Gawra, near Nineveh in northern Mesopotamia, from the Halafian period of the chalcolithic culture (c. 3800 B.C.), shows the early and universal character of the cult of the mother goddess. (*University Museum, Philadelphia*)

Marble head of the goddess Ningal, from Ur (2300–2200 B.C.). Ningal was an earth goddess concerned with childbirth and maternal functions. (*University Museum, Philadelphia*)

Sumerian seal showing the sun god Shamash (Utu) rising from the mountain (2200 B.C.). Shamash helped Gilgamesh slay Humbaba, keeper of the sacred forest, but later informed him that he would never find immortality. (*British Museum*)

The goddess Astarte at a window. Ivory inlay from Khorsabad, Assyria (8th–7th century B.C.). The mother goddess represents—as in all cultures—the three aspects of womanhood as wife and mother, lover and mistress, and chaste and beautiful virgin. (*Oriental Institute, University of Chicago*)

Part of Tablet XI of the Gilgamesh epic containing the Assyrian account of the deluge in cuneiform (c. 650 B.C.). Utnapishtim was granted eternal life when he built a ship to carry the seed of all living things and survived a great flood sent by the gods. (*British Museum*)

Clay tablet giving the Babylonian version of the creation. From Nineveh (7th century B.C.). According to this legend, Marduk, the supreme deity of Babylon, slew the water goddess Tiamat and cut her body into two pieces, from which he made the heavens and the earth. (*British Museum*)

Limestone relief slab with the goddess Ishtar (7th century B.C.). Ishtar is the Akkadian equivalent of Innana, the Sumerian queen of heaven and goddess of love. She is standing on the back of a lion, holding a harp in her right hand and a ring and rod—symbols of divinity—in her left. (*The Metropolitan Museum of Art, Rogers Fund, 1951*)

Painted limestone statue of an Egyptian scribe holding a roll of
papyrus. From Sakkara (Fifth Dynasty, 2500–2350 B.C.). Although
the Egyptians' profound sense of cosmic order seemingly ruled out
variety of interpretation, differing concepts of the same myths co-
existed, and even one priest or scribe could have varied and contradictory views about the same subject. (*The Louvre*)

Bronze statuette of Maat, Egyptian goddess of truth and justice. She is wearing a wig and an ostrich feather, symbol of truth. Pharaohs were not mortals, but gods, and were the embodiment of *maat*, the unchanging cosmic order of truth, goodness, and normality. (*Brooklyn Museum*)

Adoration of the sun at its rising and setting. From the Book of the
Dead, Hunefer Papyrus. Re was the chief sun god and thus the most
important deity in the Egyptian pantheon. Legends maintain that he
arose from the waters of chaos onto a primeval hill and then created
all forms of life. (*British Museum*)

Cuneiform tablet containing a letter
sent to Amenhotep IV by a Palestinian
king. From Tell el-Amarna. Amenhotep IV (reigned 1375–1358 B.C.)
changed his name to Ikhnaton when
he came to the throne and established
the new monotheistic cult of Atonism,
the worship of the solar disk. (*Cairo
Museum*)

Judgment of the dead. From the Ani Papyrus. Perhaps the most familiar subject from Egyptian art, this scene shows the heart of the deceased being weighed against the feather of truth. If they balanced, and the man's deeds had been worthy, Osiris, god of the dead, granted him immortality. (*British Museum*)

The sky goddess Nut, arched as the heavens, supported by the air god Shu, with the earth god Geb at his feet. From the Deir el-Bahri Papyrus (10th century B.C.). After Shu lifted Nut from the earth, she gave birth each morning to the sun and each evening to the stars. (*British Museum*)

Black marble nude figure of the sky goddess Nut. From Thebes (Twenty-Sixth Dynasty, 663–525 B.C.). Nut was the mother of Osiris and was called "the Great Lady who gave birth to the gods, the Mistress of the Two Lands." (*British Museum*)

A page from the hieratic text of the "Tale of Two Brothers," D'Orbiney Papyrus 10183 (c. 1225 B.C.). Reminiscent of the story of Joseph and Potiphar's wife in the Book of Genesis, this story tells of a man unjustly accused of seducing his brother's wife. (*British Museum*)

Plaque showing the god Baal. From Ras Shamra. The struggle of
Baal for kingship is the chief theme of Ugaritic mythology. With
the aid of the goddesses Astarte and Anath, Baal finally overcame
his rivals Yamm and Mot and established a reign of peace. (*The
Louvre and Claude Schaeffer*)

Female figure in lead from Alishar Hüyük, Anatolia, 2000 B.C. The position of the arms indicates that they probably held the breasts. The mother goddess was a permanent tradition in Anatolia, the birthplace of the Hittite culture. (*Oriental Institute, University of Chicago*)

LEFT: Figure of Astarte on a gold pendant. From Beisan, Palestine (15th century B.C.). The goddess of sexual activity, fertility, and war, Astarte volunteered to entreat the dragon Yamm to have mercy on the gods and goddesses and lighten their burdens. (*The University Museum, Philadelphia*)

RIGHT: Gold pendant with relief of Astarte standing on a lion. From Ras Shamra (15th century B.C.). When Yamm responded to Astarte's plea with an offer to become his mistress, Baal was enraged. Astarte had the divine artisan Kothar make two flying axes with which Baal might defeat the dragon. (*The Louvre and Claude Schaeffer*)

Seal showing the goddess Anath. From Ras Shamra. Anath continually helped Baal in his quest for the throne. When he was finally successful, Anath remembered the fickleness of his people and began a wild rampage of slaughter. (*The Louvre and Claude Schaeffer*)

Clay tablet containing a portion of the legend of Aqhat. From Ras Shamra. When Aqhat refused to return a bow to Anath, she became enraged and, when her orders were misunderstood, had him killed. For seven years after this, the land was cursed with drought. (*The Louvre and Claude Schaeffer*)

Mythological beast from Carchemish. The hieroglyphic texts from
Carchemish contained the sacred writings of the Hittite Empire and
posed a problem of decipherment for scholars. After two generations
of epigraphy, much progress has been made in understanding them.
(*British Museum*)

Clay tablet containing magic rituals against pestilence. From Boghazköy. More than ten thousand cuneiform tablets were found in
the royal archives at Boghazköy, the capital of the Hittite Empire.
Most were written in the Indo-European language called Kanesian.
(*British Museum*)

An architectural fragment showing a Hittite devotee worshipping. From Mar'ash (9th–8th century B.C.). Hittite kings were the chief priests in the cult of the goddess as well as being military and judicial leaders. (*The Metropolitan Museum of Art, purchase 1891*)

Alabaster cylinder showing the sun god emerging from the gates of the east. From the vicinity of Lake Van, Persia (c. 2000 B.C.). Arinna, the sun goddess in the Hittite pantheon, surpassed in importance all the other deities, including the sun god himself. (*The Metropolitan Museum of Art, purchase 1886*)

one of whom, it turned out, knew me. He gave me food and drink and I went with him and his men.

"One tribe helped me on to another until I came to Byblos, and from there to Kedem, where I lived for a half a year. The prince of Upper Retenu sent for me with the message, 'Live with me so that you may hear the speech of Egypt.' Some of his retinue had been in Egypt and knew of me. 'Why have you come here?' he continued. 'Has the king of Egypt died?' At first I concealed the truth but then told him that Sesostris had succeeded his father. 'Sesostris is a worthy successor. He is a wise ruler and a great warrior, maintaining the borders with his armies. His people love him and he will not smite the country that is friendly.'

"The prince said to me, 'Egypt is indeed happy and prosperous. You are far from home. While you are here I shall treat you well.' He married me to his eldest daughter and gave me the choice of all his land. It was a good land with plenty of figs, grapes, wine, honey, olives, barley, wheat, and cattle. He set me up as shcik of the tribe and I lived a life of luxury. I had many children, each one of whom was head of a tribe. I entertained any messenger who came to the country and helped many who were in need. The prince made me general of his army and I waged successful foreign conquests.

"One day a mighty warrior of the Retenu came to challenge me to combat. He claimed to be champion of the whole land and wanted to overcome me in order to take my cattle. The prince counseled with me. I said: 'I don't know this man. I have never entered his territory. This must be jealousy because he resents a foreigner coming here and gaining your favor. I am like a bull in the midst of a strange herd, like a Bedouin in the Delta. If it is combat he desires let him come on. I am a fighting bull and I like a tussle. Does he know that his fate is already determined?'

"That night I strung my bow and made ready my arrows. I drew out my dagger and polished my weapons. At dawn the people came together and spoke of nothing but the fight. They saw that the challenger was well armed and feared for my safety. He started the attack but I turned aside his arrows, which landed at my feet. Then as he attacked I shot him. He cried and fell on his face. I drove his lance into his back. The crowd cheered and the prince embraced me. Then I carried off the warrior's goods and cattle.

"So it was that I became rich and powerful in the land of the Retenu. I paid tribute to the god-king and begged him to allow me to return to Egypt. 'O king,' I wrote, 'I was once a fugitive and naked; now I possess much land and I am even known again in the palace at Thebes. O king, let my flight be forgiven, that I may be restored to the palace, that I may see once again the land where my heart dwells. To return would be complete happiness. I have offered sacrifices to God to grant me this favor. My heart suffers in spite of prosperity and I long to be in my native land and there be buried. May the king be gracious to me and may my request meet with the queen's favor. I have grown old and weak but I will be young again if I am restored to my own country.'

"His Royal Majesty received my request and sent me presents from the palace, as if to a foreign ambassador, and the royal sons wrote to me also. The decree that was brought from the king read as follows:

> Horus, Life of Births, King of Upper and Lower Egypt, Kheperkere, Son of Re, Sesostris, that liveth forever and ever. A royal decree to the henchman Sinuhe. Behold this order of the king is sent to thee to

instruct thee of his will. Although thou hast traveled through foreign lands from Kedemi to Retenu and hast passed from one country to another in accordance with thy desires, what hast thou done that anything should be done against thee? Thou has not cursed nor spoken ill in the assembly. Be it known by thee that thy queen resides in the palace with her children and enjoys good health.

Come back to Egypt that thou mayest see once again the royal residence where thou didst grow up. Leave thy riches there; when thou hast returned thou wilt live in comfort. Thou shalt have great honors. Thou hast given thought to thy age and the approaching day of burial. Thou wilt be given bandages from the hand of Tait and thou wilt be embalmed. Thy head will be painted blue and placed in a gilded case. Oxen will draw thy mummy and dancers will precede. The weepers will mourn at the door of the tomb and the tomb walls will be carved. Thou shalt not die in a strange land and be buried by Asiatics.

"When this decree was read to me I was in the midst of my tribe. I threw myself on the ground for joy and cried, 'How can this be done to one who became an exile from his native land? Surely the god-king is good to me in causing me to end my days in the palace.' I acknowledged the decree as follows:

The henchman Sinuhe to the Good God, King of the Two Lands, Lord of Thebes, Lord of Amon, Beloved of Re, Horus, and Hathor, all the gods of Egypt. May the gods give thee happiness, may they give thee eternity, everlastingness without bounds. This is the prayer of thy humble servant who is saved from a foreign land. O wise king, thy words I fear to repeat. What am I that thou shouldst take such thought of me? Thy strength extends to all lands. Behold this flight that I have made was really not planned; I had it not in my heart. I don't know how it came about. It was like a dream, as if a man of the Delta suddenly saw himself in the desert. I had nothing to fear. No authorities were after me. But I was led on to a strange land as by a predetermined plan.

I shall leave my goods in this land. As to the messenger, he will do as he pleaseth and as thou dost direct him. May the king live forever.

"I made a feast in Yaa and handed over my goods to my children. My eldest son became leader of the tribe and I gave him all my grain and cattle.

"Then I took the road to the south and came at length to the Paths of Horus at the edge of Egypt. From this point a messenger was sent to the palace with news of my approach. The king sent an officer with boats full of gifts for the Asiatics who had accompanied me to the Paths of Horus.

"We continued to Thebes, and at the palace gates four men met me and conducted me to the royal chamber. I found His Majesty on his throne in the golden reception room. I threw myself to the floor and the king did not know me. He questioned me but my spirit left me, and I was speechless. He told one of his aides to lift me up and then spoke to me. 'You have walked across deserts; you are old and weary. Do not be silent. Is it fear that makes thee speechless? Tell me your name.' I replied, 'I am afraid to speak to the Lord of Life.' Finally I summoned my courage and confessed who I was and told the king about my adventures. Before I could say more the queen and children were ushered into the hall.

"The king said, 'Behold Sinuhe, who has come back as an Asiatic, a creature of the Bedouins!' But they did not recognize me. 'It is not so!' cried the queen. The king assured them that it was.

"Then the princesses brought forth their collars, their

musical instruments, and their wands, and they danced before the king and sang:

> May thy hands prosper, O king! May the goddess Nub give life to thy nostril. All wisdom is in thy mouth. Thy cobra is on thy forehead. Thou hast delivered the poor from evil. May Re be gracious unto thee, O Lord of the Two Lands! Grant good things to this traveler, Sinuhe, born in the land of Egypt, who fled in fear of thee and the land. Does not the face grow pale of him who beholds thy countenance?

"The king responded, 'Sinuhe shall have neither fear nor dread. He shall be a chamberlain among the magistrates and nobles; he shall live in the midst of the courtiers.'

"When I left the palace the royal children gave me their hands and we went to the Two Great Portals. I was placed in the house of the royal retinue, the residence of a chamberlain, a place of coolness with fruits, and good things, clothes from the royal wardrobe, frankincense, and the finest perfumes in every chamber. All the servants were in their appointed places. Years were removed from my limbs. I was shaved and my hair dressed. I was arrayed in the finest linen and anointed with the best oil. I lay on a fine bed. Meals were brought to me from the palace and gifts from the royal children came without ceasing.

"There was built for me a pyramid of stone. The chief architect designed it and the master sculptor carved it and the sacred masons built it. All the appropriate things were placed in it. A garden was made for me. A statue of me was erected in the tomb and it was overlaid with gold. All this was ordered by the king. Such is not done for a man of low degree.

"So may I live in the king's favor until the day of my death."

The Shipwrecked Sailor

This is the story of an Egyptian Crusoe as told to a prince who has returned from an unsuccessful mission and now hesitates to report to the king. In order to encourage the prince to proceed to the palace with confidence the sailor tells him about his shipwreck on an enchanted island. Although there is no apparent allegorical or symbolic element involved, the story does have a certain literary quality and was written for educated readers. The idea of an enchanted island that arose from the waves and will sink again is the basis of a number of old legends.

"The Story of the Shipwrecked Sailor" is thought to be

*from the Twelfth Dynasty in the reign of Amenemhet I
(2000–1970 B.C.) and has survived in a hieratic papyrus
that was acquired by M. Golénischeff and is now in the
Hermitage Collection at Leningrad.*[11] *Although scholars
have attempted to read into the story allegorical interpretations, this story, like the tale of Sinuhe, is included here
on its own merits as a tale of adventure.*

A sailor said to a nobleman: "Be of good cheer, O prince,
for we have returned to our native land after many months
of travel on the sea. The mallet has been grasped, the
mooring post has been driven into the ground, and the
bow of the boat has been grounded on the bank. We have
offered thanks to the gods and we have all embraced each
other. We have returned in good health and have lost none
of our number even though we have traveled throughout
Nubia. Listen to me, O prince, wash yourself and prepare
to report to the king. Speak without faltering and with
sincerity, for a man is known by his speech.

"But first let me tell you of what happened to me once.
I was going to the mines of Pharaoh and I took a ship
that was 225 feet in length and 60 feet in width and was
manned by 150 of the best sailors in Egypt. They predicted that there would be little or no wind, but while we
were still at sea a storm overtook us and the waves were
twelve feet high. The ship went down and most of the
crew perished. As I swam in the sea a plank drifted toward
me and I lay on that. The sea bore me along and cast me
upon an island. I spent three days alone hiding in a thicket.
Then I became hungry and began to look around. I found

figs and grapes, fruit, grain, and melons. Nothing was lacking, for it was a paradise. I dug a hole in the ground and prepared a burnt offering for the gods.

"Suddenly I heard a loud noise like thunder. I thought it might be caused by a wave of the sea. The trees shook, the earth quaked, and I was afraid. I uncovered my face and found that the sound was caused by a gigantic serpent that was coming toward me. He was forty-five feet long; his body was overlaid with gold and his eyes were blue. He coiled himself up before me.

"Then he opened his mouth as I lay on my face and he said to me 'What has brought you here, little one? Who has brought you to this island? If you delay in telling me I shall cause you to vanish.' He took me in his mouth and carried me to his cave and put me down without any hurt. Here the dragon repeated his question: 'Who brought you to this island which is in the sea?'

"Then I humbled myself before him and replied, 'I was embarked for the mines by order of the pharaoh. A storm came upon us and I was carried to these shores on a plank.'

"The dragon answered, 'Have no fear, little one, and do not be sad. It is the gods who have let you live and brought you to this isle of the blessed where nothing is lacking, for it is filled with good things. You will stay with me four months. Then a ship will come from your own country and you will return to Egypt and die in your own city. I too have passed through evil fortunes. There were seventy-five of us here until a fire destroyed everyone, but I survived. But be of good cheer; you will live to embrace your wife and children and live once again in your house.'

"Then I bowed in obeisance and touched the ground before him and said: 'I shall tell the pharaoh about you and

your goodness to me. I shall bring to you the best perfumes and sacred oils and incense from the temples. I shall
relate to the king all that you have done, and your praises
shall be sung throughout the land. I shall offer sacrifices of
animals and birds for you. I shall send boats loaded with
the most costly products of the land of Egypt.'

"The dragon smiled and said: 'You have little store of
myrrh in Egypt. All you have is incense. I am prince of
Punt and all the myrrh that is there belongs to me. As to
perfume, that is the chief product of this island. When
you leave this place you will not return, for the island will
disappear beneath the waves.'

"A ship arrived in due time, as he had foretold. I climbed
a tall tree to see who might be on it. When I reported to
him I found that he already knew about it. 'Farewell,' the
dragon said, 'a safe journey home. You will see your
family once again. May my name be well received in your
city.'

"I bowed myself before him and he gave me precious
gifts of perfumes, cassia, sweet woods, kohl, incense, ivory
tusks, baboons, and apes. All these things I loaded on the
ship. Then the dragon spoke once more to me. 'You will
arrive in your country in two months. You will embrace
your children and be buried in your own tomb.' I went
to the shore and called the crew to me and we thanked
the master of the island for his kindness.

"We reached the Residence in two months as the dragon
had predicted. I presented the gifts from the island to the
sovereign, who thanked me in the presence of all the
nobles and appointed me to be one of his bodyguards.

"So you see, O prince, I have seen much and have at-
tained success in spite of my misfortunes. Give heed to
what I have said, for it is wise to listen."

Whereupon the prince replied, "Do not make yourself

out to be too wise. Does a man give food at daybreak to a bird he is going to kill during the day?" [12]

Here ends the "Tale of a Shipwrecked Sailor," which has been written according to an ancient book. It has been copied by Ameni-Amen-aa, a scribe with skillful fingers. Life, Prosperity, and Health to him!

The Tale of the Two Brothers

"The Tale of the Two Brothers" is part of the D'Orbiney Papyrus in the British Museum. It was written by a scribe named Enana who lived during the reign of Merneptah in the Nineteenth Dynasty (c. 1225 B.C.). Based on an earlier myth about Anubis and another divinity, Bata, it became in time a popular fairy tale throughout Egypt.[13]

There is a second section to the story describing the strange adventures of Bata in the Valley of the Acacia, and it is just as allegorical and fantastic as the first part is simple and realistic. It is practically incomprehensible and is therefore omitted.

This folk tale, perhaps the most earthy of all known Egyptian narratives, is reminiscent of the story of Joseph and Potiphar's wife in the Book of Genesis. Although the plot is of mythological origin, the author has transplanted the scene to a purely human setting, a shift that lends more enchantment to the story than it would have if it concerned the world of gods. This fact, however, does not keep the author from making use of supernatural and otherworldly events.

It is said that there were two brothers, the children of one father and one mother; the name of the elder was Anubis and the name of the younger, Bata. Anubis had a house and a wife, while his younger brother lived with them as a son. It was Bata who made the clothes, tended the cattle, plowed the land, and kept the books. And Bata was a farmer without equal. He came home in the evenings with the produce and wood. After eating supper he went out to the barn and slept with the cattle. In the morning he would prepare the breakfast for Anubis and his wife and then drive the cattle into the field. The cattle had good feed and flourished.

In the plowing season Anubis said to Bata, "Come, let us get the oxen ready; the ground has appeared and is in proper condition for the plow, for the inundation has sub-sided. Take seed-corn with you today and tomorrow we shall plow." Bata did everything he was told to do. The next morning the two brothers went into the fields and plowed, and were glad to get the season underway.

One day when they were in the field Anubis said to Bata,

"Run back and fetch more seed-corn." Bata did so, and when he arrived at the house he found his brother's wife seated, dressing her hair. And he said to her, "Get up and give me some seed-corn so that I may hurry back to the field. Anubis told me not to tarry." She replied, "Go yourself to the grain shed. I could go but I wish to complete dressing my hair." Then the young man went to the barn and filled a large bag with wheat and barley. Anubis' wife said, "How much have you on your shoulder?" He answered, "Three sacks of wheat and two sacks of barley." "You have great strength, Bata," she remarked. "I notice every day how strong and beautiful you are." And she desired him. She arose and took hold of him and said, "Come, let us take our pleasure and lie together. It will be to thy advantage, for I will make beautiful clothes for you."

Bata became enraged at this and said, "You have been like a mother to me and your husband like a father. You have said something that ought not to have been said and I pray you will not repeat it. As for me I shall tell no man of it." In spite of her pleading, Bata took up his load and departed. When he arrived at the field he and his brother continued their plowing.

In the evening Anubis returned to the house. Bata drove the cattle into the barn and did his chores. Anubis' wife, meanwhile, was smitten with fear because of what she had said to Bata. She took some grease and dirt and made herself appear like a woman who had been assaulted and beaten. When Anubis entered the house he found his wife lying on the floor, her dress torn. She did not get up to greet her husband but appeared to be sick.

Her husband said to her, "Who has done this to you?" She replied, "No one has been here except your young brother. When he came to get the seed-corn he found me sitting alone and he said to me, 'Come, we will take our pleasure and sleep together.' But I would not listen to him and said to him, 'Am I not like thy mother? Is not thy elder brother like thy father?' Then he was afraid and angry and he beat me so that I would not report it to you. Now if you do not kill him I will take my own life; for when he comes in the evening and I accuse him, he will deny it and will try again tomorrow."

Then the elder brother became enraged and sharpened his dagger and put it in readiness. He stood behind the stable door in order to slay Bata when he returned with the cattle. At sunset Bata loaded himself with the products of the field, as he always did, and returned to the barn. The first cow to enter the stall turned to Bata and said, "Be careful! Your brother is waiting behind the stable door to slay you. Flee while you can."

Bata looked under the door and saw Anubis' feet. He set his load on the ground and ran as fast as he could. Anubis followed with his dagger. Bata cried out to the god Re, "O my good Lord, thou art the judge between the evildoer and the righteous one!" Re heard his plea and caused a wide stream to appear between the two brothers, and it was full of crocodiles. So Anubis was left on one side of the river wringing his hands because he had not killed his brother.

Bata called to him from the other side, "Remain there until sunrise, and I will stand in judgment with thee before Re, for he decides who is the wrongdoer. I shall never again live with thee. I shall go to the Valley of the Acacia."

When the day dawned and the sun had risen Bata spoke to Anubis. "Why do you pursue me in order to slay me without hearing my side? I am your younger brother. You are like a father and your wife is like a mother to me. Now when you sent me to get seed-corn, it was your wife who said to me, "Come, let us spend an hour sleeping together! Your wife has turned the thing around and reversed the facts." So he told Anubis what had really happened. "As for you, you have followed to kill me with your dagger on the word of a filthy whore." Bata then took from his side a knife, cut off his privy member, and threw it into the water. Then he became faint and fell to the ground. Anubis became sorrowful, cursed himself, and wept over his younger brother, but he could not cross the stream to help him. Bata shouted to him, "Behold you were ready to remember something bad about me. Go back and tend your cattle. I shall go away to the Valley of the Acacia. Now you can do something for me. If I fall into danger you will receive a sign and come and save me."

So Bata went to the Valley of the Acacia and Anubis to his own house. As soon as he arrived he slew his wife and cast her to the dogs and sat mourning for his younger brother.

The Doomed Prince

Except in the case of the discoveries made by Bernard P. Grenfell, Arthur S. Hunt, and Sir Flinders Petrie, we know next to nothing of the places of origin and the discovery of the most valuable Egyptian papyri. This is true of the Harris 500 from the Eighteenth Dynasty that is now in the British Museum. Apparently it was complete when purchased by A. C. Harris in the middle of the nineteenth century but was partly destroyed in an explosion in Alexandria. The papyrus contains two stories—one describing the taking of Joppa by Tahuti, a general of Thutmose III; the other, a mythical story of the Doomed Prince.[14]

This papyrus breaks off toward what seems to be the end of the story, leaving the reader with the task of finishing in his own mind the fateful tale. If the story does have a hidden meaning, it would seem to be that the role of fate or destiny was by the Eighteenth Dynasty becoming a part of the Egyptian consciousness, whereas formerly life was usually taken in stride with little or no deterministic thought.

There was once a king who was sad because no son had been born to him. He prayed to the gods that he might have an heir and they said his prayer would be answered. So he slept with his wife, and in due course she bore him a son. When the Hathors came to decree his destiny they said, "He shall die either by the crocodile, the serpent, or the dog." Those who were present and heard this announcement were alarmed and told the king.

The king feared greatly and because of the decree had a house built for his son. This house was richly furnished and contained all that a person could possibly need. The boy was instructed not to go outside.

When the child grew up he went one day to the roof of the mansion and happened to see a dog following a man along the road. He asked his attendant what it was that was following the man. When he was told that it was a dog, the prince said he would like to have one. The king was told of his desire and rather than displease him he bought him a young dog.

Later on, when the boy became older, he grew restless and said to his father, "Why am I kept a prisoner? I know

I am destined to die by one of three beasts. God knows what is best for me. So why not follow my heart's desires?"

The king consented, and he was given a chariot with provisions and a servant to accompany him. He was taken across the river to the east bank and told, "Now you are free to go wherever you like."

He set out for the north, his dog following him, and he lived on the best game of the desert. Finally he arrived at the home of the chief of the Naharin. The chief had only one child, a daughter. For her he had built a house with windows seventy cubits from the ground. The chief had assembled all the sons of the chiefs of Syria and said to them, "Whoever climbs to my daughter's window shall have her as his wife."

The household of the chief of the Naharin took the prince in, treated him with great kindness, and took care of his horse. They asked him where he was from and he answered, "I am from Egypt and am the son of an official there. My mother died and my father took another wife who has been hateful to me. So I left home." Then they embraced the prince and asked him to stay with them.

One day he asked the young men what they were doing. They told him they were climbing to reach the window of the chief's daughter and thus win her for a wife. Then the prince decided to try himself, for he had seen the face of the girl from a distance and he desired her.

The next day he tried to reach the window and was successful. The chief's daughter embraced him and kissed him. Those who watched the contest ran to the father with the news that one of the youths had reached his daughter's window. The chief inquired who had achieved this difficult feat and was told that it was the son of an official in Egypt. The chief swore that his daughter was not going to be married to a fugitive from Egypt. "Let him return to his own country," he said.

The messengers went to the prince and told him what the chief had said. But the maiden clung to him and vowed that if he were taken from her she would refuse to eat or drink until she died. When the chief was informed of this he sent a messenger to slay the prince immediately. But the maiden prevented him and swore, "By the great gods, if he is slain, I shall die. If I am parted from him, I shall take my life."

When her words were reported to the father he sent for her and the prince. The young man was afraid, but the chief had had a change of heart and, embracing him, said, "Tell me about yourself, for you are now as a son to me." The prince replied, "I am the son of an official in Egypt. When my mother died, my father took another wife and she mistreated me, so I left home and came here." Then the chief gave the prince his daughter in marriage. He also gave him a fine house with servants, land, and cattle.

After several months had passed the prince said to his wife, "I am fated to die by a crocodile, a serpent, or a dog." Naturally she was greatly disturbed, and she replied, "Let your dog be killed." He said, "I cannot do a thing like that, for I have brought him up from the time he was just a puppy."

One day the prince decided he wanted to go back to Egypt on a visit. His wife feared for his safety, so she insisted on going along. They came to a town situated on a river and found a place in which to stay. The owner of the house owned a crocodile but he kept him bound. When night came the prince lay down on his couch and fell asleep. His wife had placed a bowl of milk by his side and sat near him. Suddenly a serpent came out of a hole and made for the young man, but his wife protected him. The serpent drank from the bowl, became drunk, and went to sleep on its back. The wife took her dagger and killed the serpent.

The prince awoke and his wife said, "See, you have been delivered from one of your fates. Surely you will be saved from the others." After that the prince made sacrifices to Ra and praised him.

A few days later the prince took a walk with his dog. While chasing wild game, the dog plunged into the river. The prince followed him. Out came the crocodile, who seized him and carried him off. As he bore him along, the crocodile said to the prince, "I am your fate and I have been pursuing you and . . . ."

The Eloquent Peasant

This document relates how a peasant, after being robbed, sought and found justice—an uncommon achievement for the time. On the other hand, there must have been in that period—the Middle Kingdom (2445–1580 B.C.)—already a growing feeling for human rights and social justice, for the story was apparently a popular one. However, its popularity stemmed more from its elegant rhetoric than from its content, which took the form of a monotonous series of complaints. Its elegant expression seemed to illustrate the saying of a famous contemporary, Ptah Hotep, that "goodly discourse is more hidden than the precious green-

95

stone, and yet it is found with slave-girls over the mill-stones."

Other sayings of Ptah Hotep admonished men in high positions to deal justly and impartially with all people, especially the poor. As to the farfetched expressions and flowery words of the peasant's complaints, they may not have sounded unusual to an Egyptian who had an ear for such language. Most countries have passed through a period of euphuism in literature. The setting of the story is in the reign of Nebkaure, king of Egypt in the twenty-first century B.C.[15]

In the salt country there lived a peasant named Khunanup who made his living by trading in salt and other products. One day he said to his wife, "I am going down to Egypt for food. See how much corn we have in the barn." She did this and found that they had eight bushels. He said, "Take two bushels for yourself and the children. With the other six make bread and beer for me for the journey."

The peasant loaded his asses with salt and all kinds of plants and set out for Egypt. On the way to Herakleopolis he had to pass through the domain of Rensi, the Lord High Steward, son of Meru. He encountered a servant of the estate, who was standing on the canal bank. When this workman, whose name was Dehutinekht, saw the peasant with his asses, he said to himself, "I wish I had some trick by which I could steal this man's goods and his asses."

The path was narrow and lay between the water and a field of barley. He had only to spread a shawl or a sheet over the road to compel the peasant to drive his asses either over the cloth, over the field of grain, or into the canal. He sent for a sheet and spread it across the path, ostensibly to dry.

When Khunanup came along, the workman said, "Wait there, my man. Do you intend to drive your beasts over my sheet?" Khunanup said, "No, I shall drive around it." So he drove his asses through the barley. Then Dehutinekht said, "What, do you drive your beasts over my barley?" The peasant replied, "I have no choice. You have blocked the path with your sheet, and I cannot drive them through the canal."

While they were thus arguing, the peasant's asses ate some of the barley, whereupon the workman cried, "Behold! Your animals are eating my barley. I will take your beasts to make you pay for this."

This made Khunanup angry and he shouted, "This is plain robbery. You forced me to go through the field, and because my animals ate a mouthful of grain you are going to have me punished. I know the lord of this estate. He is Rensi, the High Steward, son of Meru. He punishes all robbers in this territory and I shall go to him."

"Do you think that he will hear the complaint of a nobody like you?" asked the workman. Then he took some branches and beat the peasant severely and drove the asses away into a field for safekeeping. Khunanup wept and begged him to restore his property. Dehutinekht told him to keep his peace or he would send him to the Demon of Silence; but the peasant continued to complain of the treatment he had received. After beseeching his tormentor for a whole day, he knew it was hopeless and decided to go to Herakleopolis to see the Lord High Steward, Rensi. When he arrived at the estate he found Rensi boarding a boat to go to the judgment hall.

Khunanup bowed before the Lord High Steward, told

him he had a grievance to lay before him, and begged that a servant be sent to hear him on the matter. Rensi granted his request and sent for one of his attendants. The peasant told the messenger how he had been deceived by Dehuti-nekht and then robbed of his animals and beaten severely. In due time this was told to the Lord High Steward, who demanded that the case be brought before the council.

The nobles present said, "Let the peasant bring a witness, and if he proves his case it may be necessary to fine this Dehutinekht for what he has done." The Lord High Steward said nothing.

When Khunanup was given permission he addressed the Lord High Steward as follows: "O High Steward, my Lord! Greatest of the great, leader of all that is and all that is not. If you go to the Lake of Truth, may you sail with favorable winds. May you encounter no storms; may your sails not be torn or your mast broken; may you not be carried away by the current; may no misfortune overtake you; may you be successful in catching fish and fowl.

"You are father to the orphan, husband to the widow, brother to the rejected, and protector of the motherless. There is no guile or baseness in you. You are the enemy of wrong and the friend of the right. I know you will hear my plea and deal justly with me. I know you will avenge the wrong done to me. Behold I am weak and in misery."

Rensi went before the king and said, "I have come across a peasant who is very eloquent. He is making his plea before me because he has been robbed by a man in my service. I am sure you would enjoy hearing this peasant."

The king answered, "If you wish me good health, hold him here indefinitely without making any settlement, but keep him talking. Then have his speech brought to me, for I would like to read it. But make provision for his wife and children; one of my servants will go to their assistance. Provide also for the peasant himself."

So they gave the peasant four loaves of bread and two jugs of beer each day and also provided for his family.

Then Khunanup made a second appeal and said to Rensi, "O High Steward, my Lord. I would like to trust in your sense of justice just as we all trust in the stability of the earth and the sun in their regularity. It doesn't behoove one in your position—a dispenser of justice—to vacillate; it is not fitting that one who protects the poor should take from them. It is disillusioning to learn that one who condemns evil performs evil."

The High Steward interrupted Khunanup's argument, reminding him that he might be sent to prison for such accusations. But the peasant continued, "What a society! What are we coming to? He who measures out grain for others, keeps some for himself. He who should preserve order, commits violence. Merchants deal in false balances and deceitful weights. The leader of men acts kindly toward others only in order to receive kindness himself. You yourself, O High Steward, are like a boatman who ferries across only him who has the fare. You are like a businessman who has no charity but thinks only of selfish gain. You should not plunder a poor man whose property is his very life. You have been appointed to judge between two men, to punish the robber and recompense the robbed; but you have become the supporter of the thief."

The Lord High Steward commanded that the peasant be whipped by two men, well knowing that this would provoke another outburst of eloquence for the king's enjoyment. The next day, as Rensi anticipated, Khunanup came before him for the third time.

"O Lord High Steward," he resumed, "you continue to err. You hear but you do not heed. You are like a watchman who steals, like an administrator who lies. If you are blind to the doings of the wicked, who will punish the criminal? You are supposed to be a dam for those in danger lest they drown, but you have become for them an overflowing lake. Some day it will go ill with you in spite of your power."

Again the peasant was beaten severely, but he came before Rensi for the fourth time. "O Lord High Steward! Men put their trust in you; do not become a transgressor. You have been trained for justice and mercy, not for plunder and rapaciousness. You have been appointed to judge with impartiality, a peer of Thoth."

Khunanup appeared before Rensi nine times, endeavoring with all manner of speech to open the ears of the magistrate. "O Lord High Steward," he concluded, "you are the instrument of the god of wisdom, a judge representing the gods. One must conduct himself accordingly, dispensing justice in truth. Justice and truth are from the gods and are eternal. A man's goodness lives after him; it does not go with him to the grave. A judge's balance is his tongue; he weighs the evidence and prescribes punishment for the evildoer and freedom for the righteous one. Behold I have been appealing to you, but you have been insensitive to my cause. Now I will go to Anubis, the god of the dead, and seek justice at his hands."

Khunanup walked away, but Rensi sent two guards to bring him back. The peasant thought that they were going to imprison him because of his complaints and he said, "I crave death just as a thirsty man craves water or a baby reaches after milk. I am now ready."

But to his amazement, when he was again brought before Rensi, the Lord High Steward said, "Do not fear, peasant. We have arranged for you to live with me." To this Khunanup replied, "I shall gladly eat your bread and drink your beer, O Lord High Steward."

Then Rensi said, "Come this way to hear your petitions." So he had the petitions read from a roll of papyrus. The papyrus was sent to King Nebkaure, who was greatly pleased, and he said, "Give me your final judgment, Rensi."

Rensi sent for the peasant and also Dehutinekht, the man who had robbed him. When they were brought into the presence of the king, an inventory was made of all Dehutinekht's property—his pigs, his donkeys, his cattle, his grain fields, and his servants. All these possessions were given to the peasant, who, with his family, moved into the palace of the Lord High Steward and became Rensi's overseer.

UGARITIC-CANAANITE MYTHS

UGARITIC-CANAANITE PANTHEON

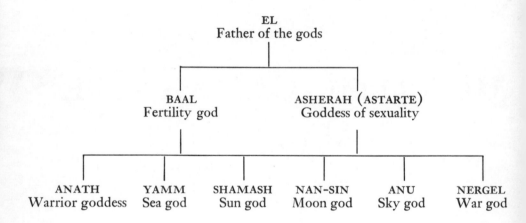

EL
Father of the gods

BAAL
Fertility god

ASHERAH (ASTARTE)
Goddess of sexuality

ANATH
Warrior goddess

YAMM
Sea god

SHAMASH
Sun god

NAN-SIN
Moon god

ANU
Sky god

NERGEL
War god

NOTE

Since the Ugaritic and Hittite people adopted foreign gods (mostly Babylonian), the indigenous deities are few and their relationships uncertain. Levels indicate importance, rather than genealogical descent, of gods.

The Importance of Ras Shamra

Some of the most important documentary discoveries in the history of archaeology have been made by unknown peasants who have not had the remotest idea of what they were finding. The Amarna Tablets were found by an illiterate woman digging for fertilizer in a field. The Dead Sea Scrolls were first come upon by a poor goatherd looking for a lost goat. In March 1928 a peasant farmer was plowing his field near Minet el Beida in Syria when he struck a large, flat stone. Upon removing the stone, he found an underground passage that led to a tomb. He made off with some artifacts, which he sold to an antique dealer.

The find came to the attention of the French authorities, who were quick to send an expedition to the site. Charles Virolleaud, a prominent Assyriologist, explored the tomb and found some potsherds, which were examined by René Dussaud of the Louvre. From an inspection of these fragments he concluded that the tomb was part of a Mycenaean burial ground, although it was on Semitic soil.

In 1929 a fully-equipped expedition headed by Claude Schaeffer began excavations at the Minet el Beida necropolis. His first campaign uncovered a variety of objects that established the ancient city of Ugarit as an important international center in the latter half of the second millennium B.C. The treasures consisted of Phoenician, Egyptian, Minoan, and Syrian statues of gods and goddesses, as well as vases, jewelry, and jars. But the remains showed a predominantly Mycenaean influence. Surrounded on the east by Palestine and Mesopotamia, on the south by Egypt, on the north by the Hittites, and on the west by the Mycenaean Greeks and Minoans, Ugarit was at the very center of western civilization at its birth. Ugarit itself was the capital of the small Ugaritic Kingdom that occupied the northwest corner of Canaan, the home of the Phoenicians and Hebrews. It was found that Ugarit had strong connections with the Hittites, the Hurrians, the Phoenicians, and the early Greeks. Ugarit was thus located at the crossroads of the Near East in the period just before the flowering of Israel and Greece, and, as the Ugaritic language shows, greatly influenced the vocabulary and ideas of both.

Schaeffer's excavations at Ugarit (modern Ras Shamra) assumed great importance later in 1929 when he discovered a tell with five distinct cultural strata. The outstanding find here was a royal library containing dozens of clay tablets. Schaeffer worked in this library every year until 1939 and then resumed in 1948. In 1955 he discovered the diplomatic archives in the palace.

The tablets were sent to Virolleaud for decipherment. They were found to be almost identical with the Amarna Tablets and were, in fact, from that period (c. 1400 B.C.). The library contained all kinds of materials—diplomatic communications, temple records, commercial transactions, administrative documents, legal and religious texts, dictionaries, bilingual tablets for scribes and priests. The texts were in eight languages, showing that this seacoast city had been truly an international center.

Important as these texts were, they were surpassed in value by other tablets that Schaeffer found in great abundance. These tablets had the same appearance as the rest but on examination they turned out to be written in an unknown language. They contained only thirty signs instead of several hundred, which meant that the script was alphabetic—and which also meant that it was pre-Phoenician and the oldest alphabet known to man! The perfection of the letters and the fact they were written in Palestinian style indicated that the script had been used in Canaan long before the coming of the Hebrews. Some alphabetic noncuneiform fragments, recently found in Palestine, are regarded as older, but the Ras Shamra alphabetic list is the oldest in cuneiform. The order of the letters is the same as the Phoenician and our own.

Without the existence of a bilingual list or glossary of any kind the task of decipherment seemed hopeless. But the discovery of some bronze axes on the same site served to initiate the work. The decipherment and identification of the language is credited chiefly to Hans Bauer of the University of Halle, Germany. His verdict that the unknown language was a western Semitic dialect related to Canaanite and Hebrew was published in 1930. He then went on to the decipherment by way of comparative analysis of the Ras Shamra signs with those of other Semitic languages. Charles Virolleaud helped make the final conclusions and began the translation of the texts.[1]

The next development was the identification of Ras Shamra with the ancient Ugarit. Not the least important result of the Ras Shamra discovery is the knowledge that the Ugaritic texts provide a linguistic backdrop for the earliest Greek and Hebrew literature.[2] In the latter part of the second millennium B.C. Ras Shamra was at the center of an international trade in which cultural ideas were being spread throughout the eastern Mediterranean countries. Along with the transmission of goods went cultic practices, religious beliefs, and the names of gods and goddesses.

The Ugaritic-Canaanite
Pantheon

If the identity and relationship of the various deities in the Ugaritic-Canaanite culture are confusing to the modern reader, they were no less uncertain to the ancients, who used their names interchangeably and assigned different gods to the same function. This tendency arose from the eclectic character of the religion of Syria and Canaan, the intellectual and commercial crossroads of the Near East.

In the Ras Shamra texts El was represented as the "Supreme Being" who inhabited the "Mount of the North"—the Ugaritic Olympus, identified variously with Mount Cassius (the modern el-Akra near Ras Shamra), Sheizer in the Orontes Valley, and Sapon, the seat of Baal after his victory over the god Mot. It was in some such lofty and remote heights that El was supposed to have exercised his cosmic duties, until he was replaced by Baal. One of the religious dramas tells us that El sired progeny from two human wives, who bore him the "Seven Good Gods of Fertility," symbolizing the seven-year cycle of plenty. The early existence of this myth-ritual drama shows that the sabbatical cycle of the Old Testament was adopted by the Hebrews from the older Canaanite culture.

Asherah originally was El's consort and is said to have borne him "the Seventy Gods." In the Ugaritic texts Baal dominates the scene, having usurped El's rule just as Marduk in Babylonia replaced Enlil. Baal was supported in his efforts to become king of the gods by Anath and Asherah, rival consorts. His main task as "exalted lord of the earth" was to control the processes of fertility, rejuvenate vegetation, and maintain the seasonal sequence. In order to achieve his position he had to kill Mot, the god of the netherworld and aridity. However, in replacing El as the chief deity of the pantheon, Baal was nowhere regarded as creator of the universe or the author of life. With the rise of the younger god Baal, El passed more or less into obscurity. Later Baal was identified with so many deities—the Semitic Hadad, the Hurrian Teshub, the Hebrew Yahweh—that the name Baal became a generic term for "lord" and was therefore used as one term of a composite deity, combining a number of functions.

The two earth goddesses Anath and Asherah played the leading roles in the Ugaritic texts describing them as rivals in their attempt to become consorts of Baal. Anath, the goddess of war and slaughter as well as of love and fertility, transferred her loyalty from El to Baal and became known as the daughter of the former and the wife of the latter. The relation of Asherah to Baal is inconsistently described; she is represented both as consort and supporter of Baal as well as bitter antagonist. Neither goddess was able to eclipse the other, so that while retaining their own identities they nevertheless served the same functions.

Much of the religious vocabulary of the Hebrews, who entered Canaan about 1200 B.C., was taken from the Canaanite and Ugaritic cultures that were already established in Palestine. El, for instance, was the chief deity of both early Israel and Ugarit. Ugaritic Baal was equated with the Hebrew Yahweh, as is seen in many Old Testament references, such as Yahweh-Baal. Gideon was called Jerrub-Baal; Saul named his son Ish-Baal; David's son was named Meri-Baal. Important locations bore the name of Baal: Baal-Hermon, Baal-Gerizim, Baal-Beer, Baal-Gad, Baal-Hazor, Baal-Meon, Baal-Peor, Baal-Perazim, Baal-Tamar. Shamash the sun god, Asherah the mother goddess, Dagon, and Anath were worshipped by the Hebrews down to the Babylonian Exile (sixth century B.C.).

In the syncretistic Canaanite period the Hebrews borrowed the worship of the goddess from those whom they conquered. The widespread worship of Ashtoreth from 1150 to 586 B.C. is attested by strong archaeological and literary evidence. It continued in spite of the antipolytheistic teachings of the prophets and later biblical redactors. Temples to Yahweh and Ashtoreth existed side by side. The veneration of Asherah is mentioned forty times in the Old Testament. It was introduced into the cultus of the royal household by Solomon, and under his son Rehoboam it became a part of the temple ritual. The importance of the Canaanite-Ugaritic goddesses Astarte (Asherah) and Anath can be appreciated from the recent discovery in all parts of Palestine of hundreds of small statues dating

from 2000 to 600 B.C. These figurines usually show a preg-
nant female with hands holding her breasts or with one
hand over a breast and the other over the genital region.

The Hebrew prophets' scathing denunciation of ritual
prostitution at the local sanctuaries of Bethel, Gilgal, Beer-
sheba, Shiloh, and Jerusalem gives some idea of how
flourishing the goddess cult was in Palestine.[3] The sacred
marriage was performed by the priestesses and their lovers
on the "beds of love" with which each shrine was equipped.
Even the Deuteronomic Reform (621 B.C.) failed to sup-
press the firmly rooted practice, and it persisted until after
the Exile.[4]

The Ugaritic idea of a mountain as the home of a god is
found frequently in the Old Testament. The sacred mountain of Ugaritic literature is called "Saphon," which, in the
Bible, is occasionally identified with Jerusalem (Ps. 48:3).
However, in the ancient world the mountain of the gods
had many locations: in Israel, Mount Sinai, Mount Ebal,
Mount Gerizim, or Mount Zion—depending on the circumstances. The role of the bull (Ugaritic "Thor"; Judges
6:25, "Hash-Shor") as a divine or sacred creature, found
everywhere in Indo-European cultures, seems to have Canaanite-Ugaritic origins.

What is most important for our purposes is that the Ras
Shamra Tablets uncovered an impressive corpus of mythology comparable to that of the Greeks. Here in existence before 1400 B.C. was an authentic Canaanite religious
and mythological literature about which nothing whatever
was known prior to 1930. Ugaritic texts, furthermore,
throw much light on many obscure passages in the Old
Testament. It is now possible to understand the prophetic
antagonism to the prevailing Canaanite religion as seen in
the rivalry of the Canaanite Baal and the Hebrew Yahweh.

We have tried to make clear that the Hebrew religion

cannot be understood apart from its Canaanite background and early environment. The Hebrews, although formally opposed to the religion of Canaan, actually adopted many of its features, particularly such cultic aspects as the fertility cult of the mother goddess, the life-death myth in agriculture, and the practice of temple prostitution. The desire of Baal for a house of his own provides a mythological precedent for the building of the temple of Yahweh in Jerusalem. "The biblical and Ugaritic accounts of the building materials (cedars of Lebanon) also link the mythical and historical houses of Baal and Yahweh respectively."[5] The Ugaritic theme of victory over chaos and the triumph of Baal is echoed in the Old Testament emphasis on the moral order and the triumph of Yahweh. Similarities exist in liturgy, seasonal feasts, the sacrificial system, and purification rites, as well as in the poetic literature of the Old Testament. The Hebrew tradition, therefore, is clearly a continuation—both by borrowing and by reaction—of its Ugaritic-Canaanite backgrounds.

The chief theme of Ugaritic mythology is the struggle of Baal for the kingship, a struggle in which he was supported by Anath, a fertility goddess. There are twelve tablets dealing with these conquests—tales filled with the bloodthirsty and sadistic activities, intrigues, and cunning deceits of the gods. The other type of Ugaritic myth has to do with human heroes. The two outstanding tablets in this category are the epics of Keret and Aqhat, which are concerned with fertility rites.

The Ugaritic myths appear somewhat obscure and abstract in their meaning because of their fragmentary character, but they are exceedingly concrete in their purpose, which was to guarantee fertility in nature and man. Thus the result of the battle of Baal, the god of fertility, and Mot, the god of sterility, decided whether the soil would be productive or dead. It was necessary, therefore, that Baal be undisputed master in the realm of the gods, although El at times was considered the supreme god. In one myth Baal had to wrest the kingship of the gods from the sea god Yamm.

In another myth the god El is the principal figure. This takes the form of a drama that describes how Dawn and Dusk and the seven gods of fertility were born through the union of El and two human wives. This myth provides the background for the sabbatical cycle in Hebrew agriculture. In other myths the consort of El is Asherah—a union that persisted in Judah down to the Exile.

The Conquests of Baal

*The twofold theme of the Baal-Anath poems is the con-
flict of the gods of fertility and sterility for the rule of the
earth and the changing seasons. The chief character is
Baal, the god of rain and fertility; the others are Yamm,
the god of the sea; Mot, the god of death and sterility; El,
the chief god of the Canaanite pantheon; and Asherah or
Astarte and Anath, rival aspirants for the position of consort of Baal.*

*The Baal-Anath story is a typical nature myth—a con-
flict between the forces of fertility and sterility, between
rainfall and drought. The primary concern of the story*

*is the cycle of the seasons, just as this is all-important to-
day throughout the Near Eastern countries, where river
and desert have always been opponents. The myth may
originally have been enacted at a seasonal festival such as
the Feast of the Ingathering, which was adopted by the
Hebrews. Such a ritual would involve the temporary death
of the king as god of the earth and his subsequent resurrection in the spring.*

*The story incorporates several themes common to all
Near Eastern folklore: the two magical weapons made for
Baal in his fight with Yamm and the inadequacy of Ashtar
as a substitute for the king because of his small stature,
thus implying that the god-king had to be taller than anyone else, strong and good-looking. Mot's invitation to
Baal to eat bread in the netherworld is paralleled in many
ancient folk tales, the idea being that once one eats of the
bread of the underworld he can never again enter the land
of man. Mot's complaint that Baal sits in comfort, "wrapped
in the garment of heaven," finds its equivalent in other
ancient literature (Ps. 104:2).*

*Most of the tablets containing the Baal-Anath stories
were found in Ras Shamra by Claude Schaeffer (1929–33).
These tablets were sketchy and incomplete, thus making
it necessary for the translators to supply many conjectural
letters and words. The one supplement to the Ras Shamra
sources is the Astarte Papyrus found in Egypt, dating
from 1500 to 1200 B.C., and now in the Morgan collection
in New York City. This substantial fragment, an Egyptian version of the Ugaritic myth, helps provide continuity
to the section on Baal and Yamm.*[6]

There was a time when no lord of the earth existed. Two gods fought for the divine kingship: Baal, the lord of the air and rain, and Yamm, the dragon of the sea. Both claimed the position and they took the matter to El, who in turn called a council of the gods and announced to them that, as far as he was concerned, the earth belonged to Yamm.

Before anyone could say anything, a young god named Ashtar stood up and offered himself as king because he was lord of the brooks and springs. But he was laughed out of court as being too young and small in stature.

A palace was built for Yamm as a sign that he was king. But Yamm proved to be a greedy king, demanding tribute from all the gods and goddesses. In desperation the gods called a council to consider what they should do about this tyrant. They decided that they were powerless to overcome the dragon Yamm. Then Astarte, rival consort of Baal, appeared and volunteered to go down to the sea and entreat the dragon to have mercy. The gods approved this plan, so Astarte removed her clothes, scented herself with rich perfumes, and went down to the sea. When the dragon heard her music, he came to the surface and inquired why she had come to him.

"I have come to entreat you," she replied, "to have mercy on the gods and goddesses and lighten their burden." Yamm was charmed by the beauty of the goddess and answered, "Goddess of beauty, if you will surrender yourself to me and become my mistress, I will ease the burdens of the gods and goddesses."

When Astarte related this to the council, Baal was enraged and went at once to the dragon, cursed him, and

challenged him to combat. Later Yamm sent his envoys to
the council to capture Baal and his cohorts, but when
they arrived they were addressed by El, the chief god,
who said he would never surrender Baal to him. He would
not consent to a combat because he knew that Yamm was
more powerful and would destroy Baal.

After the envoys left, Astarte said that no one existed
who could defeat the dragon. Even with all her weapons
she would be powerless against him.

"However," she added, "there is one way we can overcome him." She then had Kothar, the divine artisan, make
two flying axes, which, if they missed, would return like
boomerangs to their wielder. With these Baal could attack
Yamm from a distance. The artisan called the two weapons
Driver and Forger.

Baal took the axe named Driver and hurled it at
Yamm, but it missed its mark and the dragon continued
to mock him from the waters. Then he hurled the second
weapon toward the dragon. This one carried home, and
Yamm struggled to the shore, where he collapsed. Seeing
this, Baal thought Yamm was dead and he started walking
away from the scene. But Astarte shouted, "You have not
finished your job. This monster has impoverished us all
and you have not avenged us." Baal turned and saw that
Yamm was still alive. So he struck the dragon until it
seemed certain that Yamm was dead.

Baal now was king, and his first thought was that he,
too, should have a palace. Without a royal residence he
could command no respect. So he appealed to Anath for
help with El. "But," he added, "make your request through
the queen-mother Asherah. If she intercedes, the house will
be built." At this moment Anath saw that the dragon was
still alive at her feet. She beat him and drove him back into
the sea.

Then Anath prepared to present herself and her gifts to Asherah, the queen. As Anath approached the courts of heaven, Asherah feared that there must be more war among the gods and that Anath was coming to report it. But when the goddess came into her presence she saw that her mission was one of peace, for she brought gifts. The queen inquired of the goddess about her request.

Anath told her about Baal's plight—that he had no palace. The queen replied, "I will see that the artisan builds a royal house, but first we must capture the dragon so that he will not be a further hindrance." She then instructed Kothar the artisan to make a net and snare the dragon in it.

The next day the queen had her servant bring a horse, and she set out to the court of El with Baal and Anath following on foot. It was a long, tiresome journey to the Far Horizon, to the foot of the mountain of God. The two goddesses walked to the house of El, while Baal and the servant waited at the foot of the hill. Here Anath waited while Asherah entered the holy dwelling to prostrate herself before her consort, El.

"My Lord," she said, "you have seen fit to make Baal our king but he has no palace in which to reign and keep his family. I beg of you to give your permission for us to have a house built for him."

El agreed that Baal should have a house but said Baal would have to build it himself. El could not be his servant or Asherah his handmaid.

Asherah agreed to this and replied, "This Baal will gladly do. Now he will be able to act like the king of the earth and send snow and rain, drought and moisture in the right seasons."

Then Asherah came to Anath and told her to take the good news to Baal. "Tell him to send to Lebanon for its best cedars, to the mines for the finest gold and silver, and let the palace be built and beautifully furnished."

Anath did as she was instructed, and Baal sent to Lebanon and the mines for all the materials. Then he called to him Kothar the artisan. "Here is all the material," he said. "Build me a beautiful palace and place it on the Holy Mountain of the North."

"I will do as you command," said the builder, "and will also install a fine window in it."

"No," cried Baal, "I'll not have a window in my palace to let the dragon climb in and carry off my wives."

The artisan reluctantly consented but said Baal would sometime change his mind.

The palace was built and Baal invited all the gods and goddesses to a housewarming and banquet. However, even in the midst of the feasting, he had thoughts of the dragon escaping from Kothar's net and entering the palace to take revenge.

The idea so bothered him that he left his guests and went to investigate. When he came upon him he struck him a mighty blow on the head and the dragon died. Then he traveled throughout the earth, proclaiming himself king.

Upon returning to the palace Baal summoned Kothar and said, "I have killed the dragon. Now you may put a window in the palace. Whenever the window is open it will mean that we need rain. Then the windows of heaven will open and we shall have rain." Kothar said, "That was my idea and that is why I said you would change your mind."

Baal stood proudly in his palace, contemplating his kingdom and glorying in his undisputed reign over the earth. But even as he did so he suddenly thought of another rival—Mot, the spirit of death and drought, whom he had ignored. Perhaps Mot has designs upon my kingdom, he thought. He quickly sent two messengers to Mot in the netherworld with the message that his domain was in the netherworld and that he should not think about changing it.

This message was not well received by Mot. "So that's it," he cried. "Baal sits on his throne in comfort, wrapped in the garment of heaven, while I am imprisoned in this dark and filthy place. Tell your master to come down here and face me with that message. I will give him a feast to remember!"

When Baal was told this, he was afraid. So he tried to win Mot's favor by flattery and gifts. This made Mot even more enraged, and he said to the messengers, "So your master is trying to bribe me. He really must be scared. Tell him that I cannot be bribed."

It was clear to Baal that he would have to have a settlement with Mot. He took with him his clouds, winds, and rains, his servants and retinue, and prepared himself against the forces of death.

Arriving at the netherworld, Baal was invited to sit down at the banquet table. He began to eat, forgetting that anyone who ate the food of the netherworld was unable to return to the earth. Suddenly he realized that he was Mot's captive, a prisoner in the realm of the dead.

A drought immediately came upon the earth, and all vegetation began to wither. This was reported to the gods, who came down to the earth and mourned the death of Baal and the death of the soil. Anath also roamed the earth, grieving and distraught. One day, when she saw that the sun was about to go down, she said to it: "O Goddess Sun, you alone can go to the nether regions and return. When you rise again will you bring back the body of my husband for me to bury on the Mountain of the North?"

The sun did as she requested and brought back the body of Baal. Anath and Asherah carried it to the Holy Mountain and prepared for the burial. Anath entered the Court of the Gods and encountered the queen and the goddesses making merry as if nothing had happened. As for El, he too accepted the fact that Baal was dead and decided to give way no more to mourning. "We must see to a successor," he said to Asherah. "If you will name another of your sons I will appoint him king of the earth."

"He must be one who will not turn into a tyrant and mistreat the people," said the queen.

"And one who is strong, agile, and fair to look upon," added El.

After some thought Asherah came up with a suggestion. "Perhaps Ashtar would make a good king after all. Yes, let him be god of the earth."

El made Ashtar king, but when he took his place on the throne he was entirely too small and looked like a child. Nevertheless, he took over the kingship.

Meanwhile Anath went on a search for Mot. She found him in a meadow near the sea. She recalled that Mot did not know that she had brought the body of Baal from his domain, so she said, "Mot, I demand that you give me back my brother."

Mot swore that if he ever ran across Baal he would devour him. Anath left him and continued her aimless wandering. One day she ran across Mot again. This time she killed him with her sword, burned up his body in a fire, ground the bones to powder, and then scattered the dust on the earth.

That night Anath had a dream in which the earth was renewed with rain and food. This she interpreted as a sign that Baal was still alive. She went to El and reported, "I am convinced that Baal is not dead but has survived and is somewhere on the earth." El was impressed and immediately gave orders for the sun to look for him on his daily course.

It so happened that Baal had indeed been revived and,

learning of Ashtar's accession, had set out in search of him. He soon found him, beat him to death, and then re-took the throne on the Mountain of the North.

He reigned for six years and then something strange happened. Suddenly the dust and bones of Mot's body, which Anath had scattered on the earth, grew up in the soil and were joined together. Mot, in his former strength, arose again to plague Baal.

They met in battle, and it was long and fierce—first one triumphant and then the other. When it looked as if they would both drop from exhaustion, the sun saw them and cried out to Mot to cease from the battle and give up the attempt to deprive Baal of the throne, lest the gods destroy him completely.

Mot was terrified and conceded the victory to Baal. "Baal is king!" he cried.

Baal, of course, was overjoyed and resumed his reign. He expressed his gratitude to the sun in the most extravagant terms. Then the gods gathered and celebrated Baal's return to the throne with a grand banquet.

Not so with Anath. She remembered how fickle the people had been in following Mot and then Ashtar when they tried to be king. So she set out on a wild rampage of slaughter and carnage, killing everyone in sight. The earth became a sea of blood.

When Baal saw this he was not a little distressed. It grieved him to think that now that his throne was secure and the world was prosperous Anath still was determined to make war and seek revenge. He sent word to Anath that the time of warfare was past and that he was about to usher in a period of peace and goodwill on the earth. He also summoned her to his palace on the Holy Mountain.

When Anath saw the messengers approaching, she con-cluded that another usurper was on the march and that

Baal was sending to her for help. Boasting of her past conquests in his behalf, she made ready to go again to his aid. But the messengers assured her that no enemy was marching against Baal, that he was waiting for her to join him in spreading peace and goodwill among all men. "Baal urges you to hasten to the palace," the messengers told Anath, "for there he will establish a new order of peace and banish warfare from the earth."

Anath sped with the two envoys to the Mountain of the North. As they approached the Holy Hill the skies opened and lightning split the heavens and thunder reverberated across the mountains. It was a sign to Anath that Baal was truly lord of the earth and that the reign of peace had dawned.

Keret—a Ugaritic Job

The story of Baal illustrates the first type of Ugaritic myth, which deals with deities. The second class of Ugaritic myth has to do with human heroes. There may have been some basis in fact for these stories, but they assimilated so many features of traditional folklore that they became an integral part of Canaanite religious and mythological thought, particularly related to the fertility ritual. The desire for fecundity in both the soil and the human body is the dominant theme.

The dependence of the story of Keret upon traditional lore, as found in the Old and New Testaments, is seen in *the author's repeated use of the numbers seven and three. Several other elements reflect traditional lore and custom: attacking a city at dawn instead of by night (cf. Judges 9:32–33); the belief that fertility in the land depends upon the king's health (cf. II Sam. 21:1); and the transference of a disease from a person to a magical image (cf. Num. 21:6–9). The opening sentences of the story bear a striking similarity to the Old Testament book of Job.*

The legend of King Keret was one of the outstanding discoveries of Claude Schaeffer's 1930–31 Ras Shamra expedition. It was written in the fourteenth century B.C. on three clay tablets with six columns on each tablet. The reader will have to supply the ending to this legend, since the last tablet suddenly breaks off.[7]

The good king Keret lay in his inner chamber weeping and bewailing his fate. He had lost his wife, who had left him on the eve of his wedding. All his brothers had died either in war or through the plague. Worst of all, he had no son who would succeed him. Now he was afflicted with a terrible sickness.

As the king sadly pondered all this he fell asleep and dreamed. In his dream El himself appeared before him and asked him why he grieved. "Why do you weep so? Do you wish a greater kingdom? Is it greater wealth you crave?"

"No," answered Keret, "I do not crave riches or land or power. What I desire is a son who will take my throne when I am gone."

"Be no longer despondent, my son. You will have a wife

and a son. Get up, wash, prepare a sacrifice for Baal, gather together an army, make provision for a long campaign, march to the land of Udum, to the land of King Pabil, and demand of him his daughter, the beautiful Horaya."

When Keret awoke from his sleep he proceeded to do as El had commanded. He prepared a meal for Baal, assembled the army, provided food for the campaign, and then started on the march. On the third day the king with his army reached the house of Asherah, where he made a vow that he would pay a large tribute to the goddess if he gained Horaya as his bride.

Arriving at the land of Udum, they fought their way through the countryside, destroying everything in sight. On the seventh day they arrived at the castle of the king. When King Pabil saw an army drawn up before his walls he sent messengers to Keret's camp to negotiate for peace, offering silver and gold, horses and chariots, if the invaders would leave.

Keret sent back his reply: "I am not interested in riches and possessions and servants. I have come for your fair daughter Horaya and will not leave without her."

Rather than lose any of his wealth or cattle King Pabil promptly surrendered his daughter. The beautiful maiden was led to Keret's camp, followed by all the people of the castle, who sang her praises and wept.

Upon his return home, Keret made another vow to Asherah—that he would dedicate the firstborn son to her service. In honor of the marriage he gave a grand banquet, which was attended by both gods and men. Even El, the king of the gods, was there and he proposed a toast in which he prophesied that Horaya would bear Keret seven children. The banquet over, all the guests returned to their homes.

The prophecy of El came true, for in seven years Horaya bore sons and daughters. Keret forgot his vows to Asherah and spent all his time feasting and carousing. Then Asherah was provoked and decided to take vengeance on him. So she told the gods and goddesses to forsake Keret and said she would see to it that he was stricken with illness.

Shortly afterward Keret staged another banquet for his lords and ladies and all the nobility of the land. In the midst of their feasting, Horaya suddenly appeared and held up her hand for silence. When all were quiet she announced solemnly, "My lords and ladies, my tidings are not joyful but sad. It has been shown to me in a dream that our lord Keret will soon be stricken with disease. The time for celebration is past." Thereupon the guests rose and left the hall.

Asherah's spell worked, and in a short time the king was struck down with a terrible illness. Then Horaya sought out the eldest son privately and told him to go to Keret and seize the royal scepter and the kingship. Some of the sons and daughters hovered around like vultures, waiting for Keret to die so they could divide his possessions—but the youngest son, Elhau, prayed that the father would be spared. "Father," he said, "you must not die. You are a king and I pray that you will live always."

Keret replied, "My son, grieve not. Call your youngest sister, Shetmanet, that she may be present when I leave you, but do not tell her that I am sick." When Shetmanet saw her brother approaching she surmised that there was trouble at the palace. "Is our father ill?" she asked. Elhau tried to deceive her but finally admitted that the king was at the point of death. Then she wept bitterly.

They returned to the palace to find the household already in mourning. The land was smitten with drought and the people were threatened with famine. When El saw that there was no rain and that the land was withered, he called the gods together and commanded the servants of Baal to open the window of Baal's castle and let it rain. But they would not break their promise to Asherah. El pleaded with the gods to heal the king of his disease, but they were loyal to Asherah. He begged them seven times, but they said nothing.

At this El said he would resort to magic. From clay he formed an image of a dragon and gave it to Shataqat, the divine witch who removes sickness. He told her to take it to the palace of Keret. Flying over hundreds of cities and towns, she arrived at the palace and entered his chamber. She touched the king's head and caused the sickness to pass from him into the image. She washed him and restored his appetite and his good spirits.

Keret improved rapidly and commanded Horaya to bring food, which he ate heartily. After three days he was completely cured.

The sons of Keret knew nothing of his recovery. Yassib, the eldest son, came one day to the palace expecting to see the king at the point of death, but found him sitting on the throne. He could not trust his eyes but thought the king was trying to deceive his people. He was still determined to take the scepter and claim the kingship.

So he said to the king, "Father, listen to me. You have done evil. You have not acted as a good king. You are no longer capable of taking care of the needy and protecting your people. You can no longer mingle with the living. Step down from the throne, hand me the scepter, and let me reign."

Keret rose, full of vigor and might, and called down the curse of the gods upon his son. "I disown you. May the god of the netherworld break open your head. May you fall into a bottomless pit."

The Bow of Aqhat

The story of Aqhat resembles that of Keret in several features: the mingling of gods and men; the use of the number seven; the presence of Kothar, the divine smithy; the pious character of each leading figure; the fact that Daniel had no son; and the connection of death or spilling of blood with the infertility of the land.

Daniel, the father of Aqhat, is usually identified with the Daniel referred to by the prophet Ezekiel as a saintly man. The story, in fact, was earlier called "The Epic of Daniel."

Apparently the people of the ancient Near East saw in

"the heavenly bow" of Aqhat a symbol of the goddess of the chase and detected its shape in the constellation next to Orion. When the huntsman was killed and the bow lost, the land became arid; only when the hunter was resurrected and the bow restored did the earth regain its fertility. The death and resurrection of the hunter may also refer to the disappearance of Orion and its constellations from the sky and to their later restoration. The myth may have been connected with the spring festival, serving as a parable of the renewal of life. It may have been inspired in part by the ritual itself—the death and burial of the god and the period of mourning, followed by his resurrection and new life. In these rites the people used figurines of the god, which they buried and later dug up.

The incident of Daniel lying in the temple for seven days in order to gain the favor of the god is an illustration of the rite of incubation, which was common in the ancient world, especially in the Greek sanitoriums and shrines. The person desiring to gain a favor from a god or to be cured of an ailment would dress in simple clothes and sleep in the temple precincts for seven nights, during which he would have a dream or experience a divine visitation.

The direct connection between the loss of life and the infertility of the earth has been mentioned before. It is found throughout ancient literature (cf. Gen. 4:11–12 and Num. 35:33).

The story of Aqhat, like that of Keret, is a product of the French expedition during 1930–31 at Ras Shamra. Also, like the story of Keret, it is on three tablets and dates from the middle of the fourteenth century B.C.[8]

Daniel was a just and benevolent king who served his people well, but he had no son who would inherit his throne. He was grieved because of this and decided to appeal to the gods. So he took off his royal robes and put on the clothes of a beggar and went to the temple. Here for seven days he served in the daytime as a servant, and he slept at night on the roof to await a visitation of the god.

On the seventh day he received a message from El, the king of the gods, who told him to go home and embrace his wife and said that in due time he would have a son. Upon hearing this, Daniel rejoiced, dressed, and went home. For seven days his house was filled with music and dancing. He did as the god had directed, and when her time came his wife bore a son, whom they called Aqhat.

Daniel was overjoyed and exclaimed, "Now I shall have someone to look after me, to share in the good times and the bad, and to be my heir."

A few years later Daniel was sitting one day in the field when he saw a horseman approaching in the distance. As the rider drew nearer Daniel recognized Kothar, the artisan from Egypt. He was tired and dirty from the long ride, so Daniel invited him to stay and have dinner. His wife prepared a meal, and soon they were feasting on lamb and drinking wine.

When the guest departed he neglected to take his bow and arrow. Later Daniel noticed this and assumed that Kothar had left them as a token of gratitude for his hospitality. It was a beautiful bow, and Daniel gave it to his son.

Several years later, when Aqhat had grown into a handsome youth, he was in the forest hunting and met a beautiful young woman. She addressed him: "I am Anath, the goddess of the chase, and I desire that bow and arrow. In exchange I will give you silver and gold." The truth was that the bow and arrow rightfully belonged to Anath, who had ordered them made by Kothar. It was on his journey to deliver them that he had left them at Daniel's house. Aqhat, of course, was not aware of this; in fact, he did not even believe that the young woman was a goddess.

"Why don't you make your own bow?" said Aqhat. "Or, better yet, why don't you go to Kothar and have him make you one? That's his business."

This made Anath all the more determined. "I will give you eternal life," she continued. "You will live forever like El and enjoy the pleasures of the gods."

"Do not try to deceive me," replied Aqhat. "You are promising the impossible. How can a mortal being have immortality anyway? I will die when my time comes, just like anyone else. Anyhow, what does a woman want with a bow? A bow is for warriors and hunters. Or are women becoming hunters these days?"

This caused Anath to smile, but she was devising a scheme in her mind. She said, "If this is your game I can play it too. If you prefer to be arrogant and play the high and mighty you will regret it. Mark my words!"

She left him and went speedily to El, father of all gods. She prostrated herself in his presence and then proceeded to denounce Aqhat as an arrogant upstart who needed to be punished. At first El was quite indifferent to her plea and laughed it off as a trivial matter. This turned Anath into a raging, threatening goddess of war.

"Do not make fun of me!" she cried. "I am still the goddess of war and my strength is greater than yours. I can smash your head and turn your white hair to red. Then you can call Aqhat and let him try to save you from my hands."

El was too old and feeble to oppose his daughter, so he tried to pacify her. "Anath," he said, "you have always been kind and gentle and free from anger. You are probably right about this. After all, the bow is rightfully yours. Take it and do with him whatever you wish."

Rejoicing at El's change of mind, Anath quickly set out to find Aqhat. On the way she thought of another scheme. She would pretend to be a young girl out for an adventure. "Let us go hunting together," she suggested when she met him. "Meet me in the forest near the city of Abelim, where we shall have good luck." Aqhat agreed to this and Anath left him. In Abelim lived a desperado named Yatpan, who hired himself out to anyone who wanted to get rid of an enemy. Anath told him about Aqhat and he promised to take care of the matter. "After he is through hunting, when he sits down at the fire to eat and rest, I will attack him."

But suddenly Anath perceived that she had fallen in love with Aqhat and did not want to see him destroyed. All she wanted was the bow. "Wait!" she cried to Yatpan. "I have another plan. I shall disguise myself as a vulture and take you along. When the youth is eating, many vultures will circle about overhead. I shall be among them and at the right moment shall release you. You will knock Aqhat down, grab the bow and arrow, and wait for me to lift you up."

Aqhat, as they surmised, grew tired and hungry and sat down to prepare his meal. Immediately a flock of vultures appeared, circling around overhead. As the birds grew in number and became noisier Anath released Yatpan, who dropped down to attack the youth.

Apparently the ruffian had misunderstood Anath's instructions. Instead of merely knocking Aqhat unconscious, he proceeded to beat the youth until his breath left him and he lay dead on the ground.

Anath was beside herself with grief. "I have put you to death, my dear Aqhat, just for a bow! How I wish I could have you back! How foolish I have been! Now the land will become arid and there will be no fruit or wine."

As Anath was carrying Yatpan home from the dreadful scene, he dropped the precious bow and it fell into the sea, thus adding one disaster to another.

Daniel, in the meantime, sat in his court, judging the cases of his people. His daughter Paghat ran to him, shouting, "The sky is filled with vultures and the earth is withered. The crops are dried up. This can only mean that there has been a murder."

This filled Daniel with consternation and dread. "Yes, it means that for seven years Baal will curse the land with drought. There will be no rain and no relief from the heat; no grapes, no grain, no fruit."

Then Daniel told his daughter to saddle a donkey so that he could go and inspect the fields. He did so and found nothing in the vegetable patch but a bare stalk. In the grainfield he found only a withered ear of corn. He lifted his eyes to behold two of his servants running through the field toward him. "Aqhat is dead!" they cried. "Anath has done this!"

The news was almost too much for Daniel. He collapsed and for a moment could barely move. But he finally revived as he began to see why the vultures were circling above. He realized that unless he could recover the body of his son he could not bury it properly. He looked up at the birds and cursed them. "May Baal break the wings of those vultures so that they drop here at my feet. Then, if they have devoured my son's remains, I can recover them and bury them."

Baal answered Daniel's prayer with a tremendous wind, which sent the vultures hurtling to the earth at his feet. He opened the birds but found nothing. As he was about to give up, the father of all the vultures fell to the ground. Hurriedly Daniel examined his insides but found no remains of his son. But then Baal broke the wings of the mother of the vultures, and she dropped at his feet. Daniel quickly laid open her gizzards—and behold! there were fat and bone, the remains of his dead son. He buried them deep in the ground.

Then Daniel went on a hunt for the murderer of Aqhat. He visited city after city, calling down the curse of Baal upon each one if it should contain the guilty person. Finally he arrived at Abelim, where he waved his staff and cried, "Woe to Abelim if this be the city of my son's slayer!" But neither in this place did he find the murderer.

Daniel returned home and ordered a seven-year period of mourning. For seven years laments of the wailing-women were heard in the courts.

At the end of the mourning period Daniel offered a sacrifice to the gods. Paghat, his daughter, resolved to go in search of the slayer. She equipped herself with a warrior's clothing and with a sword, and, having prayed to the gods for their blessing, she went on the search.

Strangely enough, at the end of the first day when she stopped at a lodge for the night, the first man she encountered was Yatpan, although she did not know who he was. Yatpan likewise did not know who she was, but thinking she was just a traveling woman on a mission across the country, invited her to drink with him.

Yatpan was already in a drunken state, so when he indulged still more in the company of Paghat he became quite talkative and boastful. "This hand that slew Aqhat can slay thousands of foes."

Paghat, although excited inside, remained outwardly calm and served the ruffian another drink. With this his head dropped on his chest and he became unconscious. Paghat drew her sword and promptly put him to death.

THE
EPICS
OF THE
HITTITES

HITTITE PANTHEON

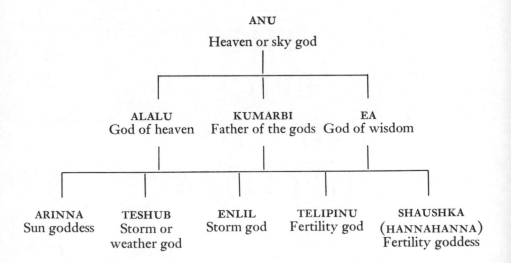

ANU
Heaven or sky god

ALALU
God of heaven

KUMARBI
Father of the gods

EA
God of wisdom

ARINNA
Sun goddess

TESHUB
Storm or
weather god

ENLIL
Storm god

TELIPINU
Fertility god

SHAUSHKA
(HANNAHANNA)
Fertility goddess

NOTE
*Since the Ugaritic and Hittite people adopted foreign
gods (mostly Babylonian), the indigenous deities are
few and their relationships uncertain. Levels indicate
importance, rather than genealogical descent, of gods.*

A Lost Empire

In 1870 the name Hittite was unknown except through a vague reference in the Bible, and that was inaccurate. Today we recognize the Hittite civilization as an important phase in the history of the ancient Near East and the Hittite people as having an established culture with a literature, a legal system, and a powerful political and military force. The Hittite Empire at its peak in the fourteenth century B.C. held sway over all of Asia Minor or Anatolia, part of Syria and northern Mesopotamia. The story of the discovery of this lost civilization by a handful of scholars is as intriguing as the stories of Sumer and Ugarit.

Many modern explorers in their journeys through Asia Minor in the middle of the nineteenth century had run across Hittite ruins and inscriptions without realizing their significance. Toward the end of the century these bits of information were put together and Hittology was born. The man chiefly responsible for the initial phase of this development was Archibald H. Sayce, an Oxford professor, who saw in the inscriptions found at Carchemish, Irviz, Hamath, Karatepe, and Boghazköy (Hattusas) an unmistakable similarity.[1] This identity in the script and art forms in such widely scattered sites could only mean there was one cultural and political unit that extended from the Aegean to Mesopotamia and Syria.

Sayce identified the Hittites with the Khatti or Heta of the Egyptian literature (Hebrew Bible: Hittim; Assyrian: Hatti). His theory was rejected by most scholars, but dramatic confirmation came surely and swiftly with the discovery in 1887 and subsequent decipherment of the Canaanite letters in which Syrian and Palestinian envoys complained to the king of Egypt about the invasion of Hittite armies. These cuneiform tablets showed that the Hittites were a great independent power in Asia Minor and that in the fourteenth century B.C. they had infiltrated Mesopotamia, Palestine, and Syria. Two of these letters were in cuneiform script but in an unknown language that was thought to be Indo-European. In 1893 a few more tablets of the same type were found at Boghazköy. These were later deciphered by the Czech scholar Friedrich Hrozný, who confirmed the surmise that they were Indo-European and called the language Kanesian.

The identification of Boghazköy as the capital of the Hittite Empire was made by a German Assyriologist, Hugo Winckler, who excavated there from 1906 to 1908. With the assistance of a Turkish archaeologist, Mackridy Bey, who worked on the site alone until 1912, he found the royal archives and unearthed more than 10,000 cuneiform tablets, most of which were written in the same Indo-European language as the two Amarna letters. Others were written in Akkadian, Hurrian, and Sumerian.

The ruins showed that Boghazköy was indeed the Hittite capital. It was several years before most of the tablets were deciphered, but at the time Winckler was able to reconstruct from some of the tablets a king list and an approximate chronology. One of the highlights of Winckler's campaigns was the discovery in the Boghazköy archives of the tablet containing the treaty drawn up between Ramses II and the Hittite king Chattusil. This was followed by the discovery of a letter of Ramses to the Hittite king concerning the treaty. As Winckler wrote at the time: "Here was confirmation that indeed the famous treaty, known from the version in hieroglyphics on the temple walls of Karnak, was also to be illuminated by the party of the second part. Ramses, identified by titles and lineage precisely as in the text of the treaty, writes to Chattusil, who is similarly identified, word for word, with certain paragraphs of the treaty." [2]

Although Hittite archaeology came to be associated with British excavators, particularly Sayce (later David Hogarth and Leonard Woolley), there were many prominent Germans in addition to Winckler: Otto Puchstein, Karl Humann, Felix von Luschau, Kurt Bittel, Ludwig Curtius, and Helmut T. Bossert. Several Turkish archaeologists were connected with later digs: V. B. Alkim, Madame H. Alkim, H. Z. Kosay, N. Özgüc, and H. Cambel.[3]

Altogether the tablets and inscriptions, the discovery of which continued steadily up until the 1950's, were written in eight languages. The problems of decipherment were complex, and it was well into the century before any appreciable progress was made. The name that stands out above all others in this connection is that of Friedrich Hrozný. As with Grotefend and Champollion before him, Hrozný proceeded by the comparative method: the identification of proper names known from inscriptions in another language. It has usually been held that an unknown language without a bilingual text cannot be deciphered. However, the refinements of comparative philology have made it possible to decipher a language, at least in part, without the aid of the parallel method.

Hrozný had before him tablets that were written in the familiar Babylonian and Assyrian cuneiform writing. Slowly but surely he was able to transfer the value of certain known ideograms to the Boghazköy documents, and he came to the conclusion that the language was Indo-European. He identified two or three words, and that was enough for a start.

Many of the Hittite tablets had been written in a borrowed language—the Akkadian. Hrozný's research now made it possible to read the tablets that were in the Hittites' own language. These in time revealed the history, laws, customs, and literary texts of the Hittites. The cuneiform tablets of Boghazköy were one thing, but a further problem emerged in the case of the hieroglyphic texts from Carchemish. It was in these inscriptions that the sacred writings were found. After two generations of epigraphy, much progress has been made in the decipherment of these texts. Among the score or more of scholars who worked on this problem, as well as on other aspects of decipherment and translation, were Ignace J. Gelb, Emil O. Forrer, Helmut T. Bossert, A. H. Sayce, F. Steinherr, Kurt Bittel, H. G. Güterbock, Albrecht Goetze, Leopold Messerschmid, J. Friedrich, and H. Otten.

As decipherment progressed after 1915 it became evident that there were mythological texts in several other languages besides the Hittite of Boghazköy. These tablets reflected the traditions of various ethno-linguistic regions of the Empire, which spread over all of Anatolia and parts of Syria and northern Mesopotamia. Briefly, these languages were Hattili or Hattic, the non-Indo-European language of central Anatolia; Nesian or Hittite, the official Indo-European tongue; the Luwian, spoken in the north; and Hurrian, the language of northern Mesopotamia and northern Syria.

Hurrian was probably the chief language in the Empire period (1800 to 1200 B.C.), when most of the scribes were of Hurrian background and came from the scribal schools of Cilicia in southeastern Asia Minor. Some Luwian words are found in the Hurrian texts and vice versa.

As Professor Güterbock points out, only the myths of foreign origin (Hurrian, Babylonian, and Canaanite) were written as literary compositions, and they are therefore called epics.[4] Local Anatolian myths were written only in connection with rituals (Hattic, Palaic, and Luwian).

The Hittite Pantheon

A pre-Hittite civilization existed in Anatolia in the Middle Bronze Age (c. 2100 B.C.).[5] The princes who established this early culture served as priests of the gods. Anittas, "the great prince" and first king (c. 1900), may have descended from this line of princes. However, the real founder of the Hittite Empire was Labarans (1680–1650), who united the city-states into a federal government and extended Hittite rule to the east and west. The imperialistic policy was further advanced by Hattusilis I (1650–1620), and under his successor Mursilis I (1620–1590) the Hittite Empire became a great Near Eastern power. Telipinu

(1525–1500) established reforms, consolidated the royal rule, and strengthened the borders against invaders.

Perhaps the best-known ruler was Suppiluliumas (1375–1335), whose reputation for military and political astuteness was so widespread that Ankhsenamon, upon the death of her husband Tutankhamon, realizing her precarious position, wrote to Suppiluliumas, suggesting that she marry one of his sons. The marriage that might have united the royal houses of Hatti and Egypt never came to pass. The Hittite king did send one of his sons, but he never reached Thebes! Either Ay or Horemheb, both aspirants to the throne, probably saw to that. Suppiluliumas conquered the Mitanni and extended the Empire to the borders of Lebanon. Mursilis II (1334–1306) not only preserved the political unity but advanced the cultural life of Hatti. He left some important religious and literary documents.

The Hittite kings, in addition to their military and judicial leadership, were the chief priests in the cult of the mother goddess. Unlike the pharaohs of Egypt, they were not considered divine in their lifetime, but in their priestly role they were thought to possess influence with the gods. Mursilis II, for instance, sacrificed to the god Telipinu to secure health for the people and fertility for the crops and animals. King Hattusilis II was the high priest of the storm god Nerik, the son of the sun goddess.

The queen also exercised priestly functions. She was the priestess of the mother goddess and could perform the sacrifices in her husband's absence. The queen wielded considerable influence in affairs of state. The wife of Hattusilis III was so powerful that he conspired to have her put out of the way.

The priestly function of the king occupied much of his time, as we have learned from royal documents. He presided at the sacrifices and rituals connected with the seasonal festivals, and at times the queen assisted. The "Great Festival of Purulli" at the vernal equinox especially demanded his presence. Here he prayed to the god of fertility for the health and prosperity of the royal family and the people at large. The spring festival resembled the Egyptian drama of Osiris and the Babylonian fertility pageant of *Enuma Elish*. The return of Telipinu from his hiding place guaranteed eternal life for the king and fertility in the land. Any offense to the gods or neglect in the performance of the king's sacerdotal function might result in some disaster to the people or the land.

The power of the Hittite kingship was all-inclusive and absolute, an authority shared to a great extent by the queen. Since the well-being of the land and its people was dependent upon the health of the king and his correct performance of the sacred duties, he had to observe many taboos and safeguards in his role as priest. The dominance of the deities over the king and people is attested in the Hittite and Hurrian myths.

The principal figure in the Hittite pantheon was the sun goddess Arinna, who as a goddess of fecundity surpassed in importance all other deities, including the sun god himself. She was, in fact, addressed in masculine terms as the "sun god of heaven." The chief designation of her husband, the sun god, was "weather god of Hatti," and as such was responsible for the fertility of the land—a function shared with his wife. Because of Hurrian influence the Hittite sun goddess was merged with the chief goddess of the Hurrians, and as the Empire reached its greatest power, the sun goddess Arinna was identified with all local goddesses somewhat in the same manner as the localization of Amon in Egypt.

In the resulting syncretism of the Hittite pantheon there

was much overlapping of functions and interchanging of names. Shaushka, for instance, was a goddess of sexuality and love and yet it was Hannahanna who became the goddess of fecundity and the equivalent of the Phrygian Magna Mater. Hannahanna was the "queen of heaven" who sent a bee to rescue Telipinu and thus restore fertility to the land. The Hittite weather god, husband of the sun goddess Arinna, was equated with Teshub, the chief god of the Hurrian pantheon.

In the Anatolian theogony the triad Anu, Alalu, and Kumarbi corresponded to the Sumerian Anu, Alalu, and Enlil. Kumarbi, the chief god of the Hurrians and rival of Anu for the throne, was known as the "father of the gods."

It is clear that throughout the ancient Near East the dominant theme controlling all religious thought was the drama of nature—the concern for fecundity, ritualized by the death of the agricultural god and his restoration by the mother goddess, who personified procreation and new life. It is also clear that the gods became composite and that even within one culture there was an overlapping in names and functions. As a result of this syncretism and interchangeableness of deities, the Ugaritic and Hittite myths are often highly confusing.

The God Who Vanished

There are several Hittite versions of the myth about the god who disappeared, each one differing in the name of the god and in the details of the story. This variation is probably due to the fact that the myth was connected with a ritual and was not considered a classical literary epic. Unlike the mythical protagonists of other cultures, the god or king in the Hittite epics does not die but just disappears.

The connection of the disappearance of the god of fertility with the barren condition of the earth is encountered in the myths of other anicent peoples, such as the stories of Tammuz in Babylonia, Adonis in Syria, and Persephone

*in Greece. As with these ritual myths, Telipinu's absence
was lamented by reciting the story at the festival of wailing. At such ceremonies the evil spirits were exorcised in
order to restore life to the earth in the new agricultural
year. In like manner Yom Kippur of the Hebrews was
ushered in by banishing the scapegoat—a ceremony by
which priest, people, and sanctuary were cleansed (Lev.
16). The idea has survived in the modern festivals of
New Year's Day and, in a symbolic way, in spring house-
cleaning.*[6]

*Another motif prominent in the literature of practically
all ancient cultures is that of the bee. In the Hittite story
the bee sent by the sun god in search of the absent Telipinu wakens Telipinu with its sting and purifies him with
its wax. The belief that the sting of the bee could cure
certain ailments and that its wax was a purifying agent
was, in fact, a common tradition.*[7] *In the extrabiblical work*
The Life and Confession of Asenath, Wife of Joseph
*(Old Testament Pseudepigrapha), the Egyptian princess
is purified and given immortality by the use of honey.*

The god Telipinu,[8] angry because of the evil on the earth,
flew into a terrible rage. He was so infuriated he put the
left sandal on his right foot and the right sandal on his
left foot. Then he stalked off into the countryside and
disappeared.

As a result the whole earth became arid. Rivers dried
up; fruit, vegetables, and grain were no more; trees and
grass withered away; men died of hunger; cattle no longer
bred.

The sun god, seeing the desolation on the earth, called all the gods and goddesses together and explained that Telipinu had fled and that with his disappearance all good things on the earth had gone.

So the gods went in search of Telipinu. They looked everywhere but could not find him. The sun god then sent for an eagle and instructed him to search the high mountains, the deep valleys, and the rivers. The eagle did as he was told but had to report failure.

The situation now became grave, for the cattle were dying and there was no food. Something had to be done. The god of the winds volunteered to make a search. He was more thorough than the rest but he also failed. He went to the city where Telipinu lived but the god was not there.

Finally the queen of heaven came forward. She was wise and knew that there was one creature that could do what the god of the winds and all the others could not do. She said, "We must send a bee to find Telipinu."

The other gods ridiculed the proposal and said, "You must be joking. If the great gods cannot find Telipinu, how do you think a little bee with its tiny wings can do it?" The queen said nothing but sent for the bee and instructed him thus: "Go and find Telipinu and, when you have done so, if he is sleeping sting him awake and then cleanse him with your wax."

Off flew the bee, over mountains and valleys, rivers and deserts. Just when he was well-nigh exhausted he came upon Telipinu in the village of Lihzina, sound asleep. Immediately he stung the god into wakefulness. Telipinu became furious. "How dare you disturb me when I was resting?" he shouted. In fact, he was more infuriated than he had been before. He went about destroying everything in sight. He stopped rivers from flowing and springs from bubbling up. He smashed houses, killed men and cattle.

The bee hastened back to the queen and reported, "I have found Telipinu but I shall need an eagle to help me bring him back." The goddess provided the eagle and they flew back to Telipinu, who, of course, was still in a state of fury. The eagle seized him and started back, accompanied by the bee.

Meanwhile, the queen had prepared to drive out the evil spirit in Telipinu by means of a magic spell. Maidens came bearing nectar, honey, sesame, and ointments. Kamrusepa, the goddess of magic, approached Telipinu and recited the ritual of healing. "Let this smooth cream soothe your mind, O Telipinu. Let this honey sweeten your disposition. Let this oil cleanse your body. Let this ointment put your soul at ease and put you in harmony with men and the gods and the world. Let this food and drink restore your strength and bring you grace and benevolence once again." All the gods repeated the chant.

Telipinu's anger and rage left him and he was full of peace and gentleness. Then the gods gathered around him and celebrated his restoration of mind and soul.

Life again came to the earth; the rivers coursed through the land; the trees flourished; grass became green; grain and fruits were plentiful; the mists disappeared; the sun warmed the earth; the cattle grazed upon the land. Spring came again to the earth. People cleansed their homes and prepared for the new year. To celebrate the new life and prosperity the fleece of a lamb was hung upon a pole in the court of the temple.

The Exploits of Kumarbi

⟨ornamental rule⟩

*The Hittite myths indigenous to Anatolia were connected
with rituals, an example of which we have seen in the story
of Telipinu. Most of the Hittite myths, however, are of
foreign origin and came from Hurrian and Akkadian
sources. Fragments of the Gilgamesh epic of Babylonia,
for instance, have been found at Boghazköy in Hurrian,
Akkadian, and Hittite versions, showing that the legend
came to Anatolia through the Hurrians and was adapted
by the Hittites to suit their purposes. Such was the case
with many Babylonian ideas.*

*Unlike the native Anatolian myths, those of foreign
origin are literary works and are called "songs." Their*

original setting is either northern Mesopotamia, Syria, or Canaan, and the names of the gods and heroes vary accordingly.

Perhaps the most important Hittite epic of Hurrian origins is the series of songs about Kumarbi, chief god of the Hurrians. The gods mentioned in the story are Sumerian, which means that the Hurrians borrowed the myth from the Sumerians, and the Hittites, conquering the Hurrians, took it from them. The scene for the most part is laid in the city of Nippur in Sumer.[9]

The story contains many elements common to ancient folklore. Stories involving the conception of a monster of stone, for example, appear in widely scattered cultures. The idea of a god or king reigning for a period of eight or nine years is also a widespread notion and is frequently mentioned in Greek mythology. The impregnation of Kumarbi, a male god, is duplicated in the Greek myth of Dionysius being born from the loins of Zeus. The ceremony of celebrating a birth, in which incantations are recited and rites are performed for the protection of the child, is found among ancient Babylonians and Africans. The practice of placing the child on the father's knee; the naming of the child as a consecration to some future deed or as a commemoration of something uttered by the father at the time of birth; the habit of carrying a child on the right shoulder; the phenomenal growth of a child born miraculously; the attempt to pacify a monster with music—all these customs are fairly universal in ancient folklore. Upelluri, the giant who bore the stone monster on his shoulder, was considered dumb. The idea that a giant is stupid prevails in European and Near Eastern lore. Likewise the recital of magic runes or mystic songs as a means of opening the treasures of heaven is a familiar motif in Norse and other ancient literature.

In the earliest days Alalu was king of heaven and he was served by Anu. After he had reigned nine years Anu made battle with Alalu and toppled him from the throne. Anu also reigned nine years, after which Kumarbi, his vizier, fought him for the throne. They battled furiously, and as Anu tried to get away Kumarbi bit him in the loins and swallowed some of his seed. Kumarbi boasted that he had deprived the king of his manhood but Anu laughed and said, "Do not rejoice over that because I have impregnated you with seed that will grow into three monsters. They will torment you until you take your own life. '

Kumarbi was terror-stricken and ran away so as not to be seen by the other gods. He went to Nippur to wait for the delivery of his offspring. At the end of seven months Anu commanded the monsters to come forth through Kumarbi's mouth. They refused to do that because it would injure them. So he said, "Come forth through his ears." This they also refused because it would defile them. "Well, find the place yourselves," said Anu in disgust.

Kumarbi became desperate because there was no such place, and it appeared that the monsters would never be delivered. He sought out Ea and laid the situation before him. Ea said, "Don't worry. I shall deliver them." He cut a hole in Kumarbi's side and out came the first monster. The others were still imprisoned.

Next Kumarbi, still tormented by the weight in his body, which was steadily increasing, went to a goddess who was known as a great healer. Kumarbi asked her for some medicine that would do away with the creatures within him. He was given a drug but it only made him sick.

Kumarbi again appealed to Ea, who now saw that the only method left was to have the delivery performed as if Kumarbi were a woman. So he called for a midwife and magicians, and after the spells were pronounced and the proper rites performed, from Kumarbi's loins came another infant, which they called "the god of the wind."

At this time Kumarbi set out to do battle with Anu for the throne, but, as it turned out, his own son—the god of the wind—helped Anu defeat him and Anu continued to rule.

Utterly dejected, Kumarbi decided on another scheme. He would send to the Lord of the Sea for help. By way of reply the Lord of the Sea sent his vizier to Kumarbi with an invitation to a banquet. Kumarbi accepted and after he had eaten much food and had drunk much wine, he spoke to the sea god. "Anu still reigns and all the gods of heaven are against me. I don't know how to conquer him."

Whereupon the Lord of the Sea replied: "Go to a mountain, lie upon it and drop your seed there, and a child of stone shall be born to you. Take the infant to the bottom of the sea, where you will find Upelluri, the giant who supports earth and heaven. Place the child on his right shoulder and it will rapidly grow into a giant, too. With your son's help you will some day be able to take the throne."

Kumarbi did as the Lord of the Sea had directed. He went to the top of the mountain and deposited his seed there. After several months there was a tremendous upheaval in the mountain. The goddesses came to assist in the birth. After much labor the rock gave forth a child made of black stone. The goddesses took it and placed it on Kumarbi's knee. Kumarbi fondled it and knew then that it would grow up to conquer all challengers. He called it Ullikummi.

Kumarbi sent for the Irsirra goddesses, the heavenly

maidens, and told them to take the child of stone to the sea and place it on the right shoulder of the giant Upelluri. The goddesses took the child, pausing on the way to show him to Enlil, god of Nippur, who saw that Ullikummi would become a terrible monster and some day do battle with the storm god.

Then the goddesses went to the depths of the sea and placed the child of stone on the right shoulder of Upelluri. The prophecy of the sea lord came true. The child soon grew up as far as the surface of the water and stood like a pillar. In a few weeks it reached to the floor of heaven.

The sun god looked down, caught sight of Ullikummi, and could not understand what manner of creature it was. He hurried to the storm god and told him what he had seen. They both went to Ishtar, and she joined them as they traveled to the sea to behold the monster of stone. "Who will overcome this giant?" the two gods asked Ishtar.

Ishtar was not so terrified as the others. "Do not worry about this fellow," she said. "Like all giants he is stupid. I can bring him low." She planned to charm the giant into submission; so she disrobed and, taking her musical instruments, she went down to the sea. Even as she sang and played sweet music she realized that the stone monster was deaf and sightless and was not in the least affected by the music or by her beauty. So she rejoined the other gods.

When the storm god heard of Ishtar's failure to overpower Ullikummi, he ordered all the seventy gods of heaven to prepare for battle. Then he unleashed the winds and the storms, hitched two bulls to his chariot, and rode forth. But he was no more successful than Ishtar. The stone monster withstood the attacks of all the gods and the assault of the winds, and even grew taller. The seventy gods fell into the sea and the storm god had to surrender.

Then Tasmisu approached the storm god and said,

"There is one thing left that we can do. We must go once more to Ea. It may be that he can consult the ancient tablets or give them to us to search for some answer." So the two of them journeyed to Ea. When Ea had listened to them he decided to take them to Enlil. They related to Enlil how powerful the stone monster was. But when Enlil recalled that this was the youngster whom he had held on his lap, he knew he could never oppose him.

It was plainly up to Ea. He went down to the sea and spoke to Upelluri, the giant who held up the stone monster. "Are you not aware of the burden you are carrying and its danger to all of us, O Upelluri? Don't you realize that this monster is made of black stone and reaches to heaven and no one has been able to overcome him?"

"No," replied Upelluri. "I didn't know anything about it. When the earth was separated from heaven by the magic knife I didn't know anything about it. My right shoulder is a little tired but I did not know who the giant was. I never heard of him."

Upelluri was stupid but his words were words of wisdom, after all. "Magic knife. Magic knife," Ea repeated to himself. That's the solution to our problem. He hurried to the old gods who had been present at the creation of the world. "Return to the storehouses, O ancient gods; recite the ancient mystic lines before the treasurehouse of heaven. Bring the old seals and the magic knife with which you separated the earth from the sky."

The gods brought the magic knife to Ea and, accompanied by the storm god and all the other gods, he quickly descended to the sea. Ullikummi boasted of his strength and challenged them to mortal combat. But this time it was different. With the magic knife Ea cut off the giant's feet and the storm god severed his body into many pieces. And Kumarbi never did reign over the gods.

The Storm God and the Dragon

The Hittite dragon story was a seasonal myth celebrated in a festival called Puruli. The dragon was identified with the rivers, which were feared in the spring when they flooded. The ritual of the slaying of the dragon, if enacted each year, would guarantee that the rivers would stay within their bounds.

The figure of the dragon was widely current in ancient mythology. The Babylonian Marduk overcame the demon of chaos, Tiamat; the Hebrew Daniel conquered the dragon Bel; the Indian Indra slew Vritra; and the Greek Hercules destroyed Hydra. The story of the slaying of a dragon by a hero became almost universal in world literature. In the Bible the combat with the dragon refers to the primordial struggle of the forces of chaos and order and also, in an apocalyptic sense, to the climactic battle to be fought at the end of the world (Isa. 5:9, 27:1; Ps. 74:14; Job 26:12; Rev. 12). The Book of Revelation also predicts Christ's triumph over the dragon Satan. The theme is continued into the Middle Ages and later with stories of the heroic Saint George, King Arthur, Siegfried, Tristram, and others. In many communities of modern Europe the slaying of the dragon is enacted in an annual pageant, and the dragon occupies a most prominent position in the culture of the modern Orient.

The Hittite story comes down to us in two versions, both of which are given here.[10]

OLDER VERSION

In the combat between Illuyankas the dragon and the storm god, the dragon was victorious. Immediately the storm god began to plan his revenge. He would invite Illuyankas to a great banquet and when the dragon was drunk he could overpower him. So he asked the goddess Inaras to prepare the feast and invited the gods and the dragon.

The tables were filled with delicious food and drink. As she was getting ready for the celebration, Inaras thought it desirable to have some additional aid on hand just in case something went wrong. So she went to the city and looked up a man by the name of Hupasiyas. "I want you to help in the capture of the dragon," she said. Hupasiyas refused to face the dragon unless he received some supernatural strength. Knowing that if he slept with Inaras he would gain extra strength and wisdom, Hupasiyas made this a condition of accepting the challenge. Inaras agreed, and he slept with her.

Inaras took Hupasiyas to the banquet hall and hid him. Then she went to invite the dragon. "I am giving a banquet and want you to be special guest," she said. The dragon was only too anxious to have a good meal, so he came and brought his family.

Illuyankas ate and drank until the tables were empty. He ate so much that he was swollen and ready to burst, but he managed with great effort to get up and get back to his lair. When he arrived, however, he could not get through the opening of his cave no matter how much he twisted and contorted himself.

At this moment Hupasiyas came up and tied the dragon with a rope so that the storm god was able to kill him.

Now it occurred to Inaras at this point that if Hupasiyas returned home and kissed his wife he would transmit his superhuman power and divinity to her and after that to her children. This would never do. So she built a house high on a cliff, far removed from all inhabitants. She took Hupasiyas to live there, but she was afraid that he might look out the window and see his wife and children, which would make him lonely and eager to go home. She warned him against this and then left the house.

For twenty days he refrained from going to the window. Then he became curious, and one day he opened the window and looked down into the valley below. There were his wife and children, and he longed to be with them.

When Inaras returned Hupasiyas begged to be allowed

to go home to see his family. She refused, but he persisted in his demands. It was clear that the next time she left him alone he would escape. It was also clear to her that the only solution to her problem was to kill Hupasiyas. This she did and then set the house on fire.

LATER VERSION

The storm god and Illuyankas the dragon were fierce rivals and were always fighting. In one battle the dragon overcame the storm god and plucked out his heart and eyes. This was a humiliating defeat for the storm god but he did not die. He immediately began to plan his revenge.

He went to the earth and married a woman of humble background. This woman gave him a son who, when he grew up, surprisingly enough, fell in love with the daughter of the dragon. Naturally, neither the girl nor her father knew whose son he was. When the day of the wedding arrived, the storm god said to his son, "When you go to the wedding and the father asks you what you would like for a marriage gift, say that you would like to have the heart and eyes of the storm god."

The gift was cheerfully made, so the storm god got his heart and eyes back. Feeling fit again, he resolved to go to the sea and engage Illuyankas in combat. He did so and this time was on the point of vanquishing the dragon. At the same time his son was being entertained at the home of the dragon and, hearing the noise, ran to the scene of the struggle. Suddenly he realized that he had been a tool of his father in bringing about the downfall of the dragon and had thus deceived his father-in-law and host. He called to his father, "I am with the Dragon. Kill me also!" So the storm god killed both Illuyankas and his own son.

GLOSSARY

A

ABYDOS. (Gr.)* The sacred city of Osiris in Middle Egypt.

ADAD. Babylonian god of rain and storm; Palestinian Hadad. Also known as Rammon.

ADAPA. Sumerian man-god of wisdom, sage of Eridu, a Sumerian capital; protagonist of the myth of Adapa; prototype of biblical Adam.

AKKADIAN. Semitic language used in Babylonia and Assyria and written in cuneiform characters.

AMON (Amen). Originally the god of Thebes, later chief deity of all Egypt; incarnate in the pharaohs; god of reproduction and creator of the universe; identified with the sun and called Amon-Re. Depicted with two tall plumes or ram.

ANATH. Canaanite-Ugaritic war goddess and consort of Baal.

ANI, papyrus of. Shows judgment scene from Book of the Dead.

ANSHAR. God of the upper world in Babylonian mythology; father of Anu, Ea, and Enlil.

ANU. God of heaven in Babylonian mythology; associated with the triad of Enlil and Ea (Enki); Sumerian and Akkadian sky god and head of the pantheon.

ANUBIS. (Gr.) Egyptian jackel god of the dead, who presides over the burial rites.

APSU. Babylonian primordial god of water; father of the gods.

ARINNA. Sun goddess and goddess of fecundity in the Hittite pantheon.

ASHUR. Chief god of battle in Assyrian mythology; solar deity and war god.

ASHURBANIPAL. Assyrian king, 668–626 B.C. His palace contained a great collection of clay tablets now in the British Museum.

ASTARTE. Mother goddess of Phoenicia and deity of sexual activity, fertility, and war. (Sumerian: Innana; Babylonian: Ishtar; Ugaritic: Asherah; Egyptian: Hathor and Isis; Phrygian: Cybele; Hebrew: Ashtoreth; Greek: Aphrodite; Roman: Venus.)

* (Gr.) following a name denotes Greek form of the capitalized name.

ATON (Ikhnaton, Akhenaton). Sun disk, god of the monotheistic religion of Amenhotep IV.

B

BA. In Egyptian mythology, the soul, believed to return and reanimate the preserved body.

BAAL. Generic name for numerous ancient Semitic gods; agricultural and fertility deity. Ugaritic, Canaanite, and Phoenician: Baal; Babylonian, Assyrian: Bel (Marduk).

BABYLON. City on the Euphrates, capital of the Babylonian Empire from about 2100 B.C.

BATA and ANUBIS. The two characters in the Egyptian legend "The Tale of the Two Brothers."

BOGHAZKÖY. Capital of the Hittite Empire, excavated by Hugo Winckler, A. H. Sayce, David Hogarth, and Helmut Bossert; its archives contained a treaty drawn up between Ramses II and the Hittite king of Chattusil.

BOOK OF THE DEAD. Composite text from the walls of tombs; contains prescriptions for life in the Hereafter; preserved on papyri.

BREASTED, JAMES HENRY (1865 – 1935). American Orientalist and Egyptologist; director of expeditions to Egypt and translator of ancient Egyptian literature.

BUDGE, E. A. WALLIS (1857 – 1934). English archaeologist; keeper of Egyptian antiquities at British Museum; acquired important papyri and tablets in Egypt.

C

CARCHEMISH. Hittite city on the upper Euphrates, scene of Ramses' war with the Hittites.

CASSIRER, ERNST (1874 –). German philosopher and author of studies in mythology.

D

DEMOTIC. Simplified and later form of the Egyptian hieratic writing; in use from 800 B.C. through Graeco-Roman times.

DUMUZI. Innana's husband in the Sumerian myth "Innana's Descent into Hell." Identified with Tammuz (q.v.).

E

EA (Enki). Earth and water god of the Babylonian pantheon; third of the triad with Anu and Enlil; associated with idea of creation and fructification; father of Marduk.

EL. Originally the leading

figure in the Ugaritic-Canaanite pantheon but was replaced by Baal, the agricultural deity. In the Ras Shamra texts he is pictured as the shadowy supreme being, the progenitor of the gods, living on the Mount of the North, the Ugaritic Olympus.

ENLIL. Earth, air, and storm god of Sumerian mythology; one of the prime triads with Anu and Ea. Patron of Nippur.

ENNEAD, THE GREAT. Grouping of nine Egyptian deities: Ra, Shu, Tefnut, Seb, Nut, Osiris, Isis, Seth, Nephthys.

ERMAN, ADOLF (1854 – 1937). German Egyptologist and epigraphist; founder of the scientific study of the ancient Egyptian language.

F

FAYYUM. District in Middle Egypt where valuable papyri have been found.

FRAZER, SIR JAMES GEORGE (1854 – 1941). Scottish anthropologist; author of *The Golden Bough.*

G

GARDINER, ALAN H. Contemporary English Egyptologist and lexicographer.

GILGAMESH. In Sumerian legend a king, who is the hero of the epic by the same name, which contains an account of the flood, probable source of the later biblical deluge story.

GINSBERG, H. L. Contemporary American Orientalist and translator of Ugaritic epics.

GOETZE, ALBRECHT. Contemporary American Orientalist and translator of Hittite mythological texts.

H

HATHOR. Egyptian cosmic goddess of fertility, often represented as a cow with the solar disk between her horns. The Seven Hathors were deities of fate appearing at the cradle to determine the course of the life of an infant.

HELIOPOLIS. (Gr.) Sacred city of the sun god.

HERAKLEOPOLIS. (Gr.) City of Middle Egypt.

HERMOPOLIS (Gr.) City of Thoth in Middle Egypt.

HIERATIC. Sacred writing; cursive and shortened form of the hieroglyphic writing used by the priests in ancient Egypt; in use as early as First Dynasty, around 3000 B.C.

HIEROGLYPHIC. The original pictographic writing system of the ancient Egyptians.

HORUS. Ancient Egyptian sky and sun god; son of Isis and

Osiris; depicted with the head of a hawk.

HROZNÝ, FRIEDRICH (1879–). Czech archaeologist, known chiefly as decipherer of the Hittite language from the study of cuneiform tablets found at Boghazköy.

HURRIAN. Chief language of Hittite Empire (1800–1200 B.C.). Many of the Hittite myths were borrowed from the Hurrian literature.

I

ISIS. Mother goddess of Egyptian religion and mythology; often depicted as suckling the child Horus. Identified with Hathor; goddess of fertility and wifehood. When Osiris was murdered by Seth she searched for his body.

K

KA. The Egyptian term for the force in a man that keeps him alive; the actual personality; the genius or spiritual self believed to dwell in man and survive in the tomb.

KARNAK. Site of temple of Amon complex at Thebes in Upper Egypt.

KERET. King, subject of a Ugaritic legend, the text of which was discovered by Claude Schaeffer at Ras Shamra in 1930.

KHEPRE (KHEPRO, KHEPRI). Name of the Egyptian sun god, particularly the morning sun, conceived of as a beetle; symbol of resurrection found in cartouches with the symbol for Ra, meaning "come into being," or "being born," denoted by the beetle rolling its egg in the form of a ball of dung.

KHONSU. Egyptian lunar deity, identified with Thoth; son of Amon-Ra and Mut; depicted with hawk's head.

KHNUM. Egyptian ram-headed god of Elephantine, associated with myths of creation and portrayed as a ram; fashioner of all things.

KOTHAR. Ugaritic craftsman god.

KRAMER, SAMUEL NOAH. Contemporary American Sumerologist and translator of Sumero-Akkadian cuneiform texts.

KUMARBI. Chief god of the Hurrians, subject of the most important Hittite epic.

M

MAAT. Egyptian goddess of truth and justice; depicted with an ostrich feather on her head; also the word for the unchanging cosmic order of truth, goodness, and normality.

MARDUK. God of Babylon;

head of the pantheon during the Babylonian Empire.

Mot. Ugaritic god of the rainless season and sterility, associated with the netherworld.

N

Nan-Sin. The Sumerian moon god; god of astrology and divination.

Neith. (Gr.) Virgin goddess of Saïs in the Delta; goddess of moisture and rain; associated with the arrow, symbol of lightning.

Nephthys. Egyptian goddess associated with funerary rites; sister of Isis and wife of Seth; member of the Great Ennead.

Nergel. Sumerian ruler of the netherworld; god of pestilence and death.

Nineveh. Ancient capital of Assyria situated on the Tigris, site of the palace of Ashurbanipal (*q.v.*).

Ninurta. Sumerian-Akkadian god of war; lord of the wells and irrigation.

Nut. The Egyptian sky goddess; wife and sister of Seb, and mother of Osiris and Isis. Member of the Great Ennead.

O

Osiris. Most popular of the Egyptian gods; god of vegetation, which dies and is revived by the annual inundation; Osiris was murdered by his brother Seth, was revived by his sister and wife, Isis; became god of the underworld and lord of the dead.

P

Petrie, Sir William Matthews Flinders (1853–1942). English Egyptologist and author; made excavations at many important sites in Egypt; credited with being the founder of modern archaeology and the first scientific excavator.

Pritchard, James B. Contemporary American archaeologist, editor, and author.

Ptah. Egyptian god of Memphis; "father of beginnings," architect of the universe.

Puruli. A Hittite festival celebrating the seasonal myth of the slaying of the dragon Illuyankas.

R

Ra (Re). Sun god of the Egyptians, supreme among the gods; his travels across the sky through the day and night were identified with ideas of life, death, and resurrection; he represented the power of the sun.

Ras Shamra. Ancient Ugarit in modern Syria; site of discovery in the 1930's of four-teenth century B.C. Canaan-ite literature by Claude F. A. Schaeffer. This litera-ture included many Ugari-tic-Canaanite myths written in a hitherto unknown lan-guage composed of an al-phabet of thirty letters in cuneiform.

RASSAM, HORMUZD. Co-exca-vator with A. H. Layard in discovering the twelve tab-lets of the Gilgamesh epic.

S

SARGON I. King of Babylon (2637–2582 B.C.); founder of the Semitic dynasty of Akkad; unified Sumer with capital at Agade.

SAYCE, ARCHIBALD H. (1845 – 1933). English Assyriolo-gist, founder of Hittology.

SCHAEFFER, CLAUDE F. A. French archaeologist, dis-coverer of Ras Shamra (an-cient Ugarit) in 1929. The excavation unearthed many cuneiform texts and a cunei-form alphabetic language older than any hitherto known.

SCHELLING, FRIEDRICH W. J. (1775–1854). German phi-losopher and author in the early nineteenth - century Romantic movement. Ad-vocated the theory that the myth was part of god's progressive revelation to man.

SEKHMET. The Egyptian lion-headed goddess of war.

SETH (SET). Egyptian animal-headed god of darkness, night, and evil; brother and slayer of Osiris; war god and storm god; member of the Great Ennead.

SHAMASH. Babylonian sun god; god of justice, law, and order.

SHU. Egyptian god of the at-mosphere, who supports the sky; son of Ra; brother and husband of Tefnut; god of Heliopolis; member of the Great Ennead.

SINUHE. An Egyptian noble of high rank who went into voluntary exile; his adven-tures are the subject of the most popular Egyptian tale.

SPEISER, E. A. Contemporary American Assyriologist and translator of Sumero-Ak-kadian texts.

SUPPILULIUMAS (1375 – 1335 B.C). Best known king of the Hittite Empire, which reached its peak in his reign.

T

TAMMUZ. Babylonian god of vegetation, inhabiting the netherworld; lover of Ish-tar, the Babylonian goddess of fertility.

TEFNUT. Egyptian goddess of mist; lion goddess; sister and wife of Shu; member of the Great Ennead.

TELIPINU. According to Hittite mythology, Telipinu, the god of fertility, disappeared. Immediately all vegetation ceased and the world became barren. He was found by a bee and brought back to the court of heaven by an eagle. Upon his rescue the earth took on new life.

THEBES. Capital of the New Kingdom in Egypt; site of the temples of Luxor and Karnak on the east bank of the Nile and the City of the Dead on the west bank.

THOTH. Scribe of the Egyptian gods; god of wisdom and learning; personification of reason and intelligence; arbiter between the gods of light and darkness, shown with the head of an ibis.

TIAMAT. Babylonian primordial goddess of water and mother of the gods; one of the chief figures in the Sumerian creation myth.

U

UGARITIC. Canaanite language of ancient Ugarit in Syria (see Ras Shamra).

ULLIKUMMI. The miraculous offspring of Kumarbi, chief god of the Hurrians. The child was conceived of stone, was placed upon the shoulders of the sea giant Upelluri, and grew to be a monster. He was supposed to help Kumarbi in his fight against Anu but was unsuccessful.

URUK. City in Babylonia (Sumer); home of Gilgamesh; biblical Erech.

W

WILSON, JOHN A. Contemporary American Egyptologist and translator.

WINCKLER, HUGO (1863–1913). German Assyriologist; chief excavator at Boghazköy, where he uncovered the ancient Hittite capital and discovered Hittite tablets.

WOOLLEY, CHARLES LEONARD. Contemporary English archaeologist and author. Excavations at Ur, a Sumerian capital, uncovered a flood stratum dating from about 3300 B.C.

Y

YAMM. Ugaritic god of the sea.

NOTES

INTRODUCTION:
THE NATURE AND MEANING OF MYTH

1. See John Van Seeters, "History and Myth in Biblical Interpretation," in the *Andover Newton Quarterly*, vol. 8, no. 3, p. 157.

2. See Alan W. Watts, *Myth and Ritual in Christianity* (Boston: Beacon Press, 1968), p. 2.

3. *Ibid.*, p. 21.

4. *Myth and Ritual in the Ancient Near East* (New York: 1958), p. 307.*

5. *The Intellectual Adventure of Ancient Man* (Chicago: 1946), p. 7.

*Books mentioned in the Bibliography have abbreviated citations in the notes.

6. For a series of technical discussions of the subject with an extensive list of references, see Thomas A. Sebeok, *Myth, a Symposium* (Bloomington: University of Indiana Press, 1958); also, Henry A. Murray (ed.), *Myth and Mythmaking* (Boston: 1968).

7. "The Historical Development of Mythology," in Murray, *Myth and Mythmaking*, p. 20.

8. For a detailed discussion of the similarity of myths throughout time and space, see Stith Thompson, *Motif Index of Folk Literature*, rev. ed. (Bloomington: University of Indiana Press, 1955–58); Clyde Kluckhohn, "Recurrent Themes in Myths and Mythmaking," in Murray, *Myth and Mythmaking*; G. P. Murdock, "World Ethnographic Sample," in *American Anthropologist* (1957) 59:664–668; Mircea Eliade, *Patterns in Comparative Religion* (New York: 1958).

9. "The Creation Myths of the North American Indian," in *Anthropos* (1957) 52:497–508.

10. *The Beginning: Creation Myths Around the World* (New York: 1956).

11. The legend is available in one Neo-Babylonian and two Neo-Assyrian fragments. It was first published in *Cuneiform Texts from Babylonian Tablets in the British Museum*, ed. L. W. King (London: 1896). The full text was translated and transliterated by L. W. King in his *Chronicles Concerning Early Babylonian Kings* in 1907. Later translations: R. W. Rogers, *Cuneiform Parallels to the Old Testament* (New York: 1912); George A. Barton, *Archaeology and the Bible* (Philadelphia: 1916); E. A. Speiser in James B. Pritchard (ed.), *Ancient Near Eastern Texts Relating to the Old Testament* (Princeton: 1955). The above section of the text is based on Barton's translation.

PART 1:

THE SUMERO-AKKADIAN MYTHOLOGY

1. Quoted in Henri Frankfort's *The Intellectual Adventure of Ancient Man* (Chicago: 1946), pp. 139, 149.

2. The Gilgamesh story as told here is based on selections from Old Babylonian, Hittite, and Assyrian sources as trans-

lated by E. A. Speiser in Isaac Mendelsohn (ed.), *Religions of the Ancient Near East: Sumero-Akkadian Religious Texts and Ugaritic Epics* (New York: Bobbs-Merrill Company, 1955); R. Campbell Thompson, *The Epic of Gilgamesh* (London: 1928); Peter Jensen, *Assyrisch-babylonische Mythen und Epen* (Keilinschriftliche Bibliothek, vol. 6, 1900); Peter Jensen, *Das Gilgamesh Epos in der Welt-Literature*, 1902–26; A. Schott, *Das Gilgamesh-Epos* (Leipzig, 1934); A. Heidel, *The Gilgamesh Epic and Old Testament Parallels* (Chicago: 1946).

3. Pritchard, *Ancient Near Eastern Texts*, p. 72.

4. The creation epic was first translated and edited by George Smith in his *The Chaldean Account of Genesis* (1876). The texts were further edited and translated in modern times by L. W. King in *The Seven Tablets of the Epic of Creation* (London: 1902) and *Cuneiform Texts from Babylonian Tablets in the British Museum* (London, 1896); E. Ebeling, *Keilschrifttexte aus Assur religiosen Inhalts* (1915–); Stephen H. Langdon, *Oxford Editions of Cuneiform Texts* (vol. 6, 1923–). More recent editions and translations are: Alexander Heidel, *The Babylonian Genesis* (Chicago: 1942 and 1951); Stephen H. Langdon, *The Babylonian Epic of Creation* (Oxford: 1924); E. A. Speiser, "The Creation Epic" in Isaac Mendelsohn (ed.), *Religions of the Ancient Near East* (New York: 1955). The story as told in this book is a free adaptation partially based on translations in the above volumes.

5. Speiser, "The Creation Epic," in Mendelsohn, *Religions of the Ancient Near East*. The translation of this text is in Pritchard, *Ancient Near Eastern Texts*, pp. 99–100.

6. These texts are translated and edited by E. A. Speiser in Pritchard, *Ancient Near Eastern Texts*; G. T. Clay, *Babylonian Texts*, Yale University Series, vol. 3 (New Haven: Yale University Press, 1922); R. C. Thompson, *The Epic of Gilgamesh* (1928); J. A. Knudtzon, *Die El Amarna Tafeln* (1915); Stephen H. Langdon, *The Mythology of All Races*, vol. 5, ed. John A. MacCulloch (New York: Cooper Square Publishers, 1964); E. Ebeling, *Altorientalische Texte zum Alten Testament*, 2nd ed., ed. H. Gressmann (Berlin: 1926); A. Heidel, *The Babylonian Genesis*. The present condensation is based partly on Speiser's translation in Pritchard, *Ancient Near Eastern Texts*.

7. See Stephen H. Langdon, *The Mythology of All Races*, vol. 5, pp. 177–179.

8. *Ibid.*, p. 183.

9. See Sir James G. Frazer, *Folklore in the Old Testament* (London: 1919), vol. 1, pp. 52 ff.

10. *The Oldest Stories in the World* (New York: 1952), p. 90.

11. The text of "Innana's Descent into Hell" is found in thirteen tablets excavated in Nippur and located today in the University of Pennsylvania Museum in Philadelphia and in the Museum of the Ancient Orient in Istanbul. They come from the first part of the second millennium B.C. The present adaptation is based on the Speiser translation in *Ancient Near Eastern Texts Relating to the Old Testament*. See also Samuel Noah Kramer (ed.), *Mythologies of the Ancient World* (Chicago: Quadrangle Books, 1961), pp. 106–118. In addition to Kramer's recent work, important studies have been made by Thorkild Jacobsen of the Oriental Institute of Chicago and by Muazzes Cig and Hatice Kizileyay, curators of the Istanbul collection. The newly edited tablets reveal a previously unknown conclusion to the story.

PART 2:

THE MYTHS AND TALES OF ANCIENT EGYPT

1. *Maat*: the unchanging cosmic order of truth, goodness, and righteousness. See my *History of Egyptian Archaeology* (New York: Thomas Y. Crowell Company, 1968), pp. 30, 31, 215.

2. This idea is suggested in John A. Wilson, *The Culture of Ancient Egypt* (Chicago: 1951), pp. 48–49.

3. For a discussion of the centrality of the sun and the river in Egyptian ideology see my *The First Heretic* (Boston: Beacon Press, 1961), pp. 49–61.

4. The hieroglyphic sign *Khepri* means "to become" or "to bring into being." Atum, Re, and Khepri are interchangeable names.

5. *The Ennead*: the nine gods who made up the heavenly court. This genealogical table is found in the Pyramid Texts.

6. See Samuel Noah Kramer, *Mythologies of the Ancient World* (Chicago: 1961), pp. 34–35.

7. The papyrus was first published by E. A. Wallis Budge in

Egyptian Hieratic Papyri in the British Museum (First Series. London: 1910). For more recent editions and translations see John A. Wilson, "Egyptian Myths, Tales, and Mortuary Texts" in Pritchard, *Ancient Near Eastern Texts Relating to the Old Testament*; E. A. Wallis Budge, *From Fetish to God in Ancient Egypt* (London: 1934). The present story is adapted in part from the last source.

8. *The Library of A. Chester Beatty, Description of a Hieratic Papyrus with a Mythological Story, Love Songs, and Other Miscellaneous Texts* (London: Oxford University Press, 1931). The present adaptation is based on Gardiner's translation as found in this volume.

9. *Egyptian Tales*. First Series, IV to XII Dynasties. 4th ed. (London: 1926), p. 129.

10. The available manuscripts are from the period 1800–1000 B.C. There are five papyri, the two most important of which are the B manuscript and the R manuscript. These are in Berlin and were published by Alan H. Gardiner in *Hieratische Papyrus V: Die Erzählung des Sinuhe* (Leipzig: Berlin Staatlichen Museen, 1909). Gardiner also made a significant study of the documentary evidence in 1916 (*Notes on the Story of Sinuhe*, reprinted from *Recueil de travaux relatifs à la philologie et à Parchéologie égyptiennes et assyrienues*, Vol. 22, Paris, 1916). Some seventeen ostraca have been found, one of which has been edited by J. W. B. Barns (*The Ashmolean Ostracon of Sinuhe*. London: Oxford University Press, 1952). One of the earliest translators was James H. Breasted (*Ancient Records of Egypt*, vol. 1, originally published in 1906, but recently brought out by Russell & Russell, New York: 1962). A good translation by John A. Wilson appears in Pritchard, *Ancient Near Eastern Texts Relating to the Old Testament*.

The present version is based on the translation of Adolf Erman in *The Literature of the Ancient Egyptians*, translated into English by A. M. Blackman (London: 1927).

11. English translations are found in E. A. Wallis Budge, *The Literature of the Ancient Egyptians* (London: J. M. Dent and Sons, 1914), p. 207 ff.; W. M. F. Petrie, *Egyptian Tales* (London: 1926), pp. 81 ff.; Adolf Erman, *Literature of the Ancient Egyptians*, pp. 29 ff. The present narrative is based on the last named source.

12. Probably meaning that the king will show the prince no favor, since he already has designs on his life.

13. The papyrus was brought to light by de Rougé in 1852 and has been translated by Sir Gaston Maspero, F. Ll. Griffith, Adolf Erman, E. A. Wallis Budge, John A. Wilson, and others. It was transcribed from the hieratic into hieroglyphic by A. H. Gardiner in *Late-Egyptian Stories* (Bibliotheca Aegyptiaca I. Brussels: 1932). The present version is based on Budge's translation in his *Literature of the Ancient Egyptians.*

14. The story has been translated and edited by Georg Ebers, E. A. Wallis Budge, Adolf Erman, T. Eric Peet, Flinders Petrie, Sir Gaston Maspero, and F. Ll. Griffith. Griffith's translation in *The Library of the World's Best Literature* (New York: 1902) provided the source for the present condensation.

15. The source material consists of four papyri from the Middle Kingdom: three in Berlin and one in the British Museum. They were first published by F. Vogelsang and A. H. Gardiner (Leipzig, 1908) and were later studied by Vogelsang, E. Suys, and Gardiner. Translations have been made by A. Erman, *Literature of the Ancient Egyptians*; A. H. Gardiner, *Journ. Egyptian Arch.*, IX, 1923; J. A. Wilson, in Pritchard, *Ancient Near Eastern Texts*; W. M. F. Petrie, *Egyptian Tales.* The present condensed version is based on Petrie and Erman.

PART 3:

UGARITIC-CANAANITE MYTHS

1. For definitive references on the discovery and decipherment of the Ras Shamra Tablets see the following: Max Niemeyer, *Entzifferung der Keilschrifttafeln von Ras Schamra* (Halle: 1930); Theodor H. Gaster, *Thespis* (New York: 1961); Arvid S. Kapelrud, *The Ras Shamra Discoveries and the Old Testament* (Norman, Okla.: 1963); Claude F. A. Schaeffer, *The Cuneiform Texts of Ras Shamra-Ugarit* (London: 1939).

2. The interrelatedness of Ugarit, Canaan, Anatolia, Minoan Crete, Egypt, and Greece, as well as the direct bearing of Ugaritic literature on the later Hebrew and Greek has received special attention by Cyrus H. Gordon: *Ugaritic Literature*

(Rome: 1949); *Ugarit and Minoan Crete: The Bearing of Their Texts on the Origins of Western Culture* (New York: 1966); *Ugaritic Textbook* (Rome: 1965).

3. Amos 2:7 ff., 5:4–6; Hosea 4:14 ff.; Jeremiah 3:30, 5:7; Isaiah 8:31, 52:8; Ezekiel 23:17. See also I Kings 15:12; Deuteronomy 23:17 ff.

4. For a new study of the influence of the Canaanite practices in sex worship on the Hebrew religion see Raphael Patai, *The Hebrew Goddess* (New York: KTAV Publishing House, 1967).

5. Cyrus H. Gordon, in Samuel Noah Kramer (ed.), *Mythologies of the Ancient World* (New York: 1961), pp. 205–206.

6. The existing studies of the Baal-Anath myth are written almost exclusively for specialists. The chief editions and translations are Cyrus H. Gordon's *Ugaritic Literature* (Rome: 1947), *Ugaritic Textbook* (Rome: 1947), and *Ugarit and Minoan Crete* (New York: 1966); Charles Virolleaud's articles in numerous issues of *Syria*, H. L. Ginsberg, in Isaac Mendelsohn (ed.), *Religions of the Ancient Near East* (New York: 1955), and in James B. Pritchard (ed.), *Ancient Near Eastern Texts Relating to the Old Testament* (Princeton: 1955); Theodor H. Gaster in *Iraq* (Vol. 6, 1939); W. F. Albright in *Bulletin of American School of Oriental Research* (1932, 1941); J. Obermann, *Ugaritic Mythology* (New Haven: 1948). The present modernized version is based on several translations.

7. The tablets have been edited and translated by H. L. Ginsberg, "The Legend of King Keret," in *Bulletin of the American Schools of Oriental Research* (1946) and in Pritchard, *Ancient Near Eastern Texts* (1950); C. H. Gordon, *Ugaritic Handbook*; T. H. Gaster in *Jewish Quarterly Review* (London: 1946–47). Others who have made studies of the myth are Charles Virolleaud, O. W. Thomas, J. Obermann, and F. Rosenthal. The present version is a modernized rendering based on several of the above translations.

8. It was first edited by Charles Virolleaud in *La légende phenicienne de Danel* (Mission de Ras Shamra I, 1936). Later editions and special studies were published by S. Spiegel in the Louis Ginsberg Jubilee Volume (1945); J. Obermann, *How Daniel was Blessed with a Son* (Publications of the American Oriental Society, Offprint Series, no. 20, 1946); Y. Sukenik,

"The Composite Bow of the Canaanite Goddess Anath" (*Bulletin of the American Schools of Oriental Research*, no. 107); H. L. Ginsberg, "Ugaritic Myths and Epics" in Mendelsohn, *Religions of the Ancient Near East.*

PART 4:

THE EPICS OF THE HITTITES

1. These ancient sites were in Asia Minor, Syria, and northern Mesopotamia.

2. From Winckler's "Nach Boghazköi! Ein Fragment," *Der Alte Orient*, XIV, no. 3 (1913).

3. For a comprehensive and dramatic account of the Hittite excavations, including the discoveries at Carchemish, Karatepe, and Kadesh; decipherment, and history, see C. W. Ceram, *The Secret of the Hittites*, translated from the German by Richard and Clara Winston (New York: Alfred A. Knopf, 1956).

4. S. N. Kramer, *Mythologies of the Ancient World* (Chicago: 1961), p. 143.

5. All the dates in this chapter are B.C.

6. For other examples of expelling the evil spirits and cleansing the house or temple at the beginning of the year, see J. G. Frazer, *The Golden Bough* (New York: Macmillan, 1951), pp. 555–559.

7. B. F. Beck, *Honey and Health* (New York: Robert M. McBride & Co., 1938); H. M. Ransome, *The Sacred Bee in Ancient Times and Folklore* (Boston: Houghton Mifflin Company, 1937).

8. The Telipinu myth has been edited and translated into German by H. Otten ("Die Überlieferungen des Telipinu-Mythus," *Mitteilungen der vorderasiatiech aegyptischen Gesellschaft*, Vol. 46, No. 1, 1942) and into English by Albrecht Goetze (in Pritchard, *Ancient Near Eastern Texts*); H. G. Güterbock (in Kramer, *Mythologies of the Ancient World*); and Theodor H. Gaster (*The Oldest Stories in the World*). The present version and the following stories in this section are condensed and composite ones based in part on the above editions.

9. Some forty tablets—all in poor condition—have been

assembled in the attempt to give some continuity to the story. Scholars chiefly responsible for the work of translating and editing these fragments are: E. Forrer (1936), H. G. Güterbock (1945, 1946, 1948), H. Otten (1950), and A. Goetze (1955). In order to make the story intelligible many restorations and reconstructions have been necessary.

10. Studies and translations of the story of Illuyankas the dragon have been made by T. H. Gaster (*The Oldest Stories in the World*); A. H. Sayce (in the *Journal of the Royal Asiatic Society*, 1922); H. Zimmern (*Streitberg-Festgabe*, 1924; pp. 430–41); A. Goetze (*Kulturgeschichte Kleinasiens*, 1933; pp. 131 ff.); A. Goetze (in Pritchard, *Ancient Near Eastern Texts*).

BIBLIOGRAPHY

ALBRIGHT, WILLIAM F. "New Light on Early Canaanite Language and Literature." *Bulletin of the American Schools of Oriental Research*, no. 45, February 1932.
———. "The North Canaanite Epic of 'Al 'Eyân Ba'al and Môt." *The Journal of the Palestine Oriental Society*, vol. 12, no. 4, 1932.
BARTON, GEORGE A. *Archaeology and the Bible.* 7th ed. Philadelphia: American Sunday School Union, 1937.
BREASTED, JAMES HENRY, ed. and trans. *Ancient Records of Egypt: Documents from the Earliest Times to the Persian Conquest.* 5 vols. 1906. Reprint. New York: Russell and Russell, 1962.
BROOKSBANK, F. H. *Stories of Egyptian Gods and Heroes.* New York: Thomas Y. Crowell Company, 1914.

Büchler, Adolf. *Studies in Jewish History*. London: Oxford University Press, 1956.

Budge, E. A. Wallis. *Book of the Dead: Egyptian Texts, Translation, and Vocabulary*. London: 1909.

——. *From Fetish to God in Ancient Egypt*. London: Oxford University Press, 1934.

——. *Hieratic Papyri: Texts and Translations*. London: 1910.

Campbell, Joseph. *The Masks of God: Oriental Mythology*. New York: The Viking Press, 1952.

Cassirer, Ernst. *Language and Myth*. Trans. Susanne Langer. New York: Harper & Brothers, 1946.

——. *The Philosophy of Symbolic Forms*. Trans. Ralph Manhein. New Haven: Yale University Press, 1953–57.

Ceram, C. W., ed. *Hands on the Past*. New York: Alfred A. Knopf, 1966.

——. *The Secret of the Hittites*. New York: Alfred A. Knopf, 1956.

Chiera, Edward. *Sumerian Epics and Myths*. Chicago: University of Chicago Press, 1934.

——. *Sumerian Religious Texts*. Upland, Pa.: Crozer Theological Seminary, 1924.

Childe, Vere Gordon. *New Light on the Ancient Near East*. 4th ed. New York: Frederick A. Praeger, 1953.

Colum, Padraic. *Myths of the World*. New York: Macmillan, 1930.

Cooke, Harold P. *Osiris, a Study in Myths, Mysteries, and Religion*. London: Humphries, 1931.

Daniel, G. E. *Myth and Legend*. New York: Macmillan, 1955.

Deuel, Leo. *Testaments of Time: The Search for Lost Manuscripts and Records*. New York: Alfred A. Knopf, 1965.

de Vaux, Roland. *Ancient Israel: Its Life and Institutions*. Trans. John McHugh. New York: McGraw-Hill, 1961.

Driver, G. R. *Canaanite Myths and Legends*. Edinburgh: T. Clark, 1956.

Eliade, Mircea. *Myth and Reality*. Trans. W. R. Trask. New York: Harper & Row, 1963.

——. *Patterns in Comparative Religion*. Trans. Rosemary Sheed. New York: Sheed and Ward, 1958.

ERMAN, ADOLF. *The Literature of the Ancient Egyptians.* Trans. A. M. Blackman. London: Methuen and Company, 1927.

FRANKFORT, HENRI. *Ancient Egyptian Religion.* New York: Harper & Brothers, 1961.

———. *Kingship and the Gods.* Chicago: University of Chicago Press, 1948.

———. *The Intellectual Adventure of Ancient Man.* Chicago: University of Chicago Press, 1946.

FRAZER, SIR JAMES G. *Folklore in the Old Testament.* Vol. 2. London: Macmillan, 1919.

———. *The New Golden Bough.* Ed. T. H. Gaster. New York: Criterion Books, 1959.

FRIED, JEROME, *see* LEACH, MARIA.

FRIEDRICH, JOHANN. "Ras Shamra. Ein Überblick über Funde und Forschungen." *Der Alte Orient,* Vol. 33, Nos. 1, 2. 1933. Leipzig: Hinrich'sche Buchhandlung, 1933.

GARSTANG, JOHN. *The Hittite Empire.* London: Constable, 1929.

———. *The Land of the Hittites.* London: Constable, 1910.

GASTER, MOSES. *Studies and Texts in Folklore and Magic.* 3 vols. London: Maggs Brothers, 1925–28.

GASTER, THEODOR H. *The Oldest Stories in the World.* New York: The Viking Press, 1952.

———. *Thespis.* 2nd rev. ed. New York: Doubleday & Company, Anchor Books, 1961.

GINSBERG, LOUIS. *The Legends of the Jews.* 7 vols. Philadelphia: The Jewish Publication Society of America, 1911–38.

GORDON, CYRUS H. *Ugarit and Minoan Crete.* New York: W. W. Norton and Company, 1966.

———. *Ugaritic Handbook.* Rome: Pontificio Institutio Biblico, 1947.

———. *Ugaritic Literature.* Rome: Pontificio Institutio Biblico, 1947.

GRAY, LOUIS HERBERT, ed. *The Mythology of All Races.* Vol. 12, *Egyptian,* by W. Max Muller. New York: Cooper Square Publishers, 1924.

GURNEY, O. R. *The Hittites.* Baltimore: Penguin Books, 1952.

GÜTERBOCK, HANS G. *The Art and Literature of the Hittites.* Chicago: University of Chicago Press, forthcoming.

HEIDEL, ALEXANDER. *The Babylonian Genesis*. 2nd ed. Chicago: University of Chicago Press, 1951.

————. *The Gilgamesh Epic and Old Testament Parallels*. Chicago: University of Chicago Press, 1946.

HERZBERG, MAX JOHN. *Myths and Their Meaning*. Boston: Allyn and Bacon, 1961.

HOGARTH, D. G. *The Hittites of Asia Minor*. Cambridge Ancient History. Cambridge University Press, 1931.

HOOKE, S. H. *Myth and Ritual*. London: Oxford University Press, 1933.

————. *Origins of Early Semitic Ritual*. London: Oxford University Press, 1938.

HROZNÝ, FRIEDRICH (BEDŘICH). "Hittites." *Encyclopaedia Britannica*.

JACOBSEN, THORKILD. *The Sumerian King List*. Chicago: University of Chicago Press, 1939.

JAMES, E. O. *Myth and Ritual in the Ancient Near East*. New York: Frederick A. Praeger, 1958.

————. *The Ancient Gods*. New York: G. P. Putnam's Sons, 1960.

KAPELRUD, A. S. *The Ras Shamra Discoveries and the Old Testament*. Norman, Okla.: University of Oklahoma Press, 1963.

KING, L. W., ed. *Cuneiform Texts from Babylonian Tablets in the British Museum*. London: 1896.

————. *Legends of Babylon and Egypt in Relation to Hebrew Tradition*. 1918.

————, ed. *The Seven Tablets of the Epic of Creation*. 2 vols. Semitic Text and Translation Series. London: Luzac, 1902.

KRAMER, SAMUEL NOAH. *History Begins at Sumer*. New York: Doubleday & Company, 1959.

————, ed. *Mythologies of the Ancient World*. New York: Doubleday Anchor Books, 1961. Chicago: Quadrangle Books, 1961.

————. *Sumerian Mythology*. Rev. ed. New York: Harper & Row, 1961.

————. *The Sumerians: Their History, Culture, and Character*. Chicago: University of Chicago Press, 1963.

LANGDON, STEPHEN H. *The Babylonian Epic of Creation*. Oxford: Clarendon Press, 1924.

————. *The Epic of Gilgamesh*. Philadelphia: University of Pennsylvania Press, 1917.

————. *Sumerian Texts from the Early Period*. Paris: Paul Guenthner, 1913.

————. *Tammuz and Ishtar*. Oxford: Clarendon Press, 1914.

LEACH, MARIA. *The Beginning: Creation Myths Around the World*. New York: Funk & Wagnalls Company, 1956.

————, and FRIED, JEROME. *Standard Dictionary of Folklore, Mythology, and Legend*. 2 vols. New York: Funk & Wagnalls Company, 1949–1959.

LONG, CHARLES H. *The Myths of Creation*. New York: G. Braziller, 1963.

McCARTHY, JUSTIN, ed. *The World's Great Classics*. Egyptian *Literature*. New York: The Colonial Press, 1901.

MURRAY, HENRY A., ed. *Myth and Mythmaking*. Boston: Beacon Press, 1968.

OBERMANN, J. *Ugaritic Mythology*. New Haven: Yale University Press, 1948.

PATAI, RAPHAEL, and GRAVES, ROBERT. *Hebrew Myths: The Book of Genesis*. Garden City, N. Y.: Doubleday & Company, 1963.

————. *Man and Temple in Hebrew Custom, Belief, and Legend*. New York: KTAV Publishing House, 1967.

PETRIE, WILLIAM M. F. *Egyptian Tales*. First Series. London: Methuen and Company, 1926.

PFEIFFER, C. F. *Ras Shamra and the Bible*. Grand Rapids: Baker Book House, 1962.

PRITCHARD, JAMES B., ed. *Ancient Near Eastern Texts Relating to the Old Testament*. 2nd ed. Princeton: Princeton University Press, 1955.

RANK, OTTO. *The Myth of the Birth of the Hero*. Trans. F. Robbins and S. E. Jellife. New York: Robert Brunner, 1952.

REED, WILLIAM L. *The Asherah in the Old Testament*. Fort Worth, Tex.: Texas Christian University Press, 1949.

ROGERS, ROBERT W. *Cuneiform Parallels to the Old Testament*. New York: Eaton and Mains, 1912.

SAYCE, A. H. *The Hittites: The Story of a Forgotten Empire*. London: Religious Tract Society, 1888.

SCHAEFFER, CLAUDE F. A. *The Cuneiform Texts of Ras Shamra-Ugarit*. The Schweich Lectures of the British Academy,

1936. London: British Academy-Oxford University Press, 1939.

———. "Secrets from Syrian Hills." *National Geographic Magazine.* Vol. LXIV, No. 1, July 1933.

SCHOLEM, GERSHOM. *Major Trends in Jewish Mysticism.* New York. Schocken Books, 1961.

SPEISER, E. A., trans. *Genesis* (The Anchor Bible). Garden City, N. Y.: Doubleday & Company, 1964.

SPENCE, LEWIS. *Myths and Legends: Ancient Egypt.* Boston: David D. Nickerson and Co. n.d.

SYKES, EGERTON. *Everyman's Dictionary of Non-Classical Mythology.* New York: E. P. Dutton, 1961.

THOMPSON, R. CAMPBELL. *The Epic of Gilgamesh.* Text and translation. London: Oxford University Press, 1928.

WILSON, JOHN A. *The Culture of Ancient Egypt.* Chicago: University of Chicago Press, Phoenix Books, 1951.

WOOLLEY, C. LEONARD. *Abraham, Recent Discoveries and Hebrew Origins.* New York: Scribners, 1936.

———. *A Forgotten Kingdom.* London: Penguin Books, 1953.

INDEX